Winston Churchill Biography

Lessons from a Visionary Leader

Douglas Glenn Rohde

TABLE OF CONTENTS

INTRODUCTION
The Cult of Churchill

The country's most renowned liberal historian, G.M. Trevelyan, gave a lecture to a packed Conway Hall in Red Lion Square, central London, on May 30, 1945, one month after Hitler's suicide and the liberation of Berlin by the Red Army commanders Georgy Zhukov and Ivan Konev, and twenty-one days after the German surrender ended the Second World War in Europe. In his speech, he made no mention of Winston Churchill or the Allied victory. Never once.

Rather, Trevelyan steadfastly adhered to the predetermined theme, "History and the Reader." After gaining notoriety by discrediting the idea that history could be studied as a science, he put out an alternative to what he dubbed "dryasdust" historians by highlighting the value of history as both a depiction of historical facts that were gathered through as thorough a search as possible and as literature. However, he was unable to help but nod in the direction of recent happenings and indulge in a little English haughtiness. He claimed that Britain approached history with objectivity. The world might be a more enlightened place if more people could follow its lead.

He spoke in a haughty tone and stooped manner. He proclaimed that "some nations," such as the Irish, "are too historically minded, in that they cannot get out of the past at all." He stated that "the Germans themselves" had grown up with biased, overly patriotic accounts of history. One-sided history has caused enormous harm in the modern era. It is a particularly lethal weapon when history is employed as a branch of propaganda. History as it is currently taught and written in England was the only other option. We suffer on this island right now more from ignorance of history than from misusing it.

That previous statement still holds true. Without acknowledging the interwoven histories of other peoples, English history itself cannot be comprehended. Trevelyan saw no need to justify the over-historicization of the Irish people, for example. Maybe he ought to have thought about what his fellow believer had said: "What do they know of England," Kipling moaned, "who only England knows?"

Then Trevelyan went into detail about how cultural prejudice and a lack of historical knowledge can result in the extinction of ancient civilisations (outside of Greece and Rome). Even the most famous historians had struggled with this. He illuminated Carlyle and Macaulay (his great-uncle) from his vantage point as Regius Professor of History at Cambridge and cautioned that they, too, had been hindered. How? Trevelyan concluded that they "would have been better historians if they had been through an academic course of history such as they could have got if they had lived at the end of the nineteenth century instead of at the beginning," in the words of a shop-steward of the official historian's union.

What does this have to do with Winston Churchill, you ask?

We haven't dealt with the realities of empire in the same way that we haven't dealt with our most devoted domestic gods. So far, an open confrontation with history has been avoided. Churchill received almost no attention from Trevelyan in his 900-page History of England. There are just three mentions of him: the first is as a steadfast Free Trader in Balfour's Cabinet; the second is as a Liberal Party member 'searching around for a kingdom'; and the third is in 1940, when 'England', facing supreme danger with her old courage', 'discovered the symbol in Winston Churchill'. It helps to put things in perspective that the sign was completely omitted from Trevelyan's Conway Hall speech.

Rather than a subject of intense historical scrutiny, Churchill has become a burnished icon whose cult has long been out of control. It's interesting to note that the cult maintained a low profile during the five major periods of his life: his travels abroad, the First World War, the 20-year European Civil War Armistice, the Second World War, and his final term in government. Even at the height of the Blitz, it was nothing like what Tory politicians and a layer of conservative and liberal historians would eventually transform it into.

Chips Channon describes a miserable club lunch with other Tory appeasers on the day Churchill went to shake hands at the Palace in an unreleased entry from his diaries. We have a half-breed as our

Prime Minister, Rab Butler is quoted as stating by the author. About a day later, the 1922 Committee chairman of the Tory backbenchers said that "three-quarters of his members were willing to give Churchill the heave-ho" and reinstate Neville Chamberlain, the mastermind behind the Munich Agreement with Hitler. In The Churchill Factor, Boris Johnson takes pleasure in the hostility that many Tory MPs have shown toward Churchill and expresses a strong sense of identification with his subject: "To lead his country in war, Churchill had to command not just the long-faced men of Munich - Halifax and Chamberlain - but hundreds of Tories who had been trained to think of him as an opportunist, a turncoat, a blowhard, an egotist, a He continues by quoting a letter written by Nancy Dugdale to her husband Tommy, a pro-Chamberlain MP who is currently serving in the military. She provides information on the tone of the Conservative Party.

One may also add that the manufactured affection for Churchill and the ways in which he was used came to represent the longing for a long-gone Empire that had been backed by all three major political parties and powerful labor organizations. The 'golden days' of the past are deeply ingrained in the British people's collective unconscious. His name was also cited when necessary, such as in 1982 when it was difficult to understand that the United Kingdom was really a collection of North European islands. Thatcher was re-elected and was seen as the leader of the world thanks to her war's success. Even worse, she started calling Churchill "Winston," as if she knew him personally.

Paul Addison, a social historian, agreed with Barnett that the Falklands War was crucial in reviving Churchill. In his 1980 book reviews of four new works, he made the case that the cultural and political backsliding could be attributed to Harold Wilson and Edward Heath's inability to modernize the nation in the 1960s and '70s. "At least in spirit, Churchill has outlived them, resuming his place as one of Mrs. Thatcher's household gods in British politics." However, according to Addison, those same decades had also offered a welcome breeze to clear the cobwebs: "The patriotic epic was an offense to the spirit of the age, except in the debased and self-destructive form of the Bond films." Only when anti-war sentiment and social satire were present, as in Tony Richardson's The Charge of the Light Brigade, were the traditional military-imperial spectacles deemed appropriate.

The growth of the Churchill industry, which has marketed the man as the "Yankee Marlborough," has been correlated with changes in academic and cultural objectives in the United States.

The Thatcher-Reagan economic consensus in the middle of the 1980s necessitated a political, cultural, and psychological remodelling in line with the advent of a new world order. A global marketplace for Anglophones required new stories. As a result, a great number of British documentaries, serials, and features were prepared for global distribution. According to the British cultural industry, what the American people wanted to see where costumed soap operas that exalted the pre-1945 ruling elite and cruder and more simplistic Jane Austen adaptations than the last one. Churchill started serving as the diet's daily fiber. In three different films— Churchill: The Wilderness Years, War and Remembrance, and Churchill: 100 Days That Saved Britain—British actor Robert Hardy even portrayed him.

The living Churchill, like Trevelyan, always recognized the significance of history, including his own contribution to it. He boasted cleverly, "I haven't always been wrong. History will support my claims, especially because I'll be the one to create that history. From a young age, he did this, and over the years, he continued to produce self-justifying accounts.

A small but vocal minority of decolonizers are now challenging Churchill's deification as the best imperial warlord in the early twenty-first century. If one looks at it in the long run, there is nothing particularly exceptional there. This was the fate of a number of Roman Emperors while that empire was in existence, as the ancient history expert Mary Beard noted in her regular TLS blog, "A Don's Life." Later European powers adopted it as a custom. Leopold of Belgium, whose control of and brutality in the Congo led to the murder of several million Africans, was one of the greatest villains Europe has ever produced. In the spring of 2020, during demonstrations sparked by the Black Lives Matter movement in the United States, his statues throughout Belgium were toppled. It remains to be seen whether the falling of statues is just a spasm and whether things will return, as they sometimes do, to post-imperial conformity.

Despite his prodigious talent for self-promotion, which irked his liberal and conservative colleagues greatly, Churchill ultimately did not need to "write the history myself." He would have been pleased with the weightless criticism of his few detractors as well as the dedication with which his epigones cultivated his reputation. He kept a close eye on book sales and didn't mind a little bad press if it helped sell a few copies. There was never enough money.

However, it's possible that this tolerance did not extend to criticisms of the British imperial purpose leveled against him in the past or attacks on his statue conducted by demonstrators now on English college campuses. The true religion of Churchill was imperialism. He never felt bad about it. He worshiped at its shrine even before he was made its High Priest. For him, the British Empire represented an incredible accomplishment because it had the largest collection of colonies the world had ever seen at the time.

This point of view was followed by the promotion of and faith in racial and civilizational supremacy. But Churchill regarded this and much everything else domestically and abroad through the lens of upholding and defending the Empire. When the adversaries of the British Empire were white and a part of the same "civilization," race became less important. Churchill admired the Boers' ferocity in southern Africa, but not the Pashtun tribes' resistance to the British on India's northwest frontier. He also valued the Gurkhas' mercenary skills, but only because the British had trained them as imperial auxiliary soldiers. Even if the Third Reich was terrible, it was still better than the vicious Japanese, who only started to detest once they assaulted British territory in Asia.

Churchill's political philosophy was so influenced by the empire that if British holdings, global hegemony, or economic interests were at issue, no adventure was too perilous, no crime too expensive, and no war was superfluous. The status quo would also be severely threatened by domestic upheavals and disputes. Churchill may have switched political parties whenever he wanted to advance his career, but this infrequently had an impact on his politics.

There were sacred individuals who served specific roles in several ancient religions. The role of binders was the most crucial of them because practically everything was connected to and bonded to them. Winston Churchill did not hold such a position in politics during his lifetime, with the exception of a brief window during the height of the war. Even back then, those who disagreed with him or confronted him were rarely silenced. Aneurin Bevan, a left-leaning Labour MP, had yelled, "Idolatry is a sin in a democracy," as the adulation got out of hand.

In terms of style, Churchill was frequently impetuous, always discursive, occasionally disorganized, but also possessed a peculiar vitality that made him seem fairly down to earth despite his social status. He felt equally at home in the shadowy corners of the political underground as he did at Blenheim Palace. When he was elected prime minister, Britain was in the midst of an existential crisis, and elites and commoners were deeply divided about the threat that the Third Reich posed. He had been little more than a shrewd politician trying to advance his career up the political ladder up until that point. He was willing to get his hands dirty in order to achieve this. quite filthy. Peaky Blinders, a well-liked BBC drama, featured this element of him when Churchill is shown supporting a Special Branch agent tasked with assassinating Sinn Féin sympathizers in the Midlands.

Why is there so much hatred? Reactionary politicians have existed in contemporary British history before Churchill. His haughtiness is frequently blamed for this, and maybe what infuriated people the most was that he was a boaster. He took his victories too seriously. Canning, Peel, Disraeli, Lloyd George, Keir Hardy, and Nye Bevan were all straightforward leaders that the British did not mind, but they did not enjoy it when their noses were rubbed in their own dust. Additionally, Churchill regarded his own population as adversaries on far too many instances, including at Tonypandy in 1910, during the 1926 General Strike, and in Scotland in 1919. How is it possible that this will ever be a phenomenon?

At the time, this did not turn him into a cult figure; quite the contrary occurred. He was acknowledged as a war leader, but the questions remained. People realized they had no other option by the time he took office as prime minister at the helm of a National Government with Attlee serving as deputy prime minister. As a result, they stood by him until they had the chance to get rid of him, which they did in July 1945 without any hesitation.

However, support was never guaranteed, not even during the conflict. The disaster at Dunkirk had traumatized the country when Churchill gave his famous "we shall never surrender" speech, notwithstanding the dramatics of the well praised movie Darkest Hour. It became clear at that point that the herd mentality that permeated the First World War's early years would not prevail. The men departing Dunkirk were aware of their lack of preparation, poor arming, and the fact that the ruling class was clueless as to why this had occurred. The brains of people trained to always obey their superior officers are troubled even by semi-victories.

Churchill was gushing in his praise and ecstatic at the devastation. None of this, however, had a significant impact on German morale. Cologne returned to regular operation after a fortnight.

But by 1942, the ruling class as a whole had become weary of Churchill's direction. Japan had conquered Singapore. Tens of thousands of Indians who were being used as cannon fodder had their morale affected by Gandhi and Nehru's Quit India agitation, which they had started. Subhas Chandra Bose, an ultranationalist, made the decision to form the Indian National Army, which would fight the British in India, using Indian POWs taken prisoner by the Japanese.

The inability to meet production goals at home had an impact on supplies in Britain and on the front lines. Only one-third of respondents to a Gallup poll said they were satisfied with Churchill and his war cabinet. Despite his concerns that doing so would shock the nation, the diarist Harold Nicolson wrote that some center-left leaders had urged him that "Churchill had to be brought down." Another Conservative politician's buddy, Cecil Beaton, claimed that they openly addressed Churchill's shortcomings. They responded, "Sir Stafford Cripps," when asked who might take his position. Cripps, a name that is hardly spoken now as the best leader we never had, neither Attlee nor Bevin.

There was also a clear sense of unrest among the military. Cairo hosted the now-forgotten "Forces Parliament" during 1943 and 1944. The Putney discussions between Oliver Cromwell and the Levellers served as the model for the Cairo Parliament, which was organized by troops and junior commanders to discuss the future of Britain after the war. Nationalization, banking and land reform, inheritance, and employment were all covered. In the fictitious elections, Labour won by a landslide. The Conservatives were last. The experiment was immediately terminated as was inevitable.

Given Churchill's standing in the war, it was widely believed that the Tories would win the 1945 general election. However, the editor of The Times had been foresighted. Contrary to the propaganda, anti-Churchill sentiments had persisted throughout the war, especially in working-class neighborhoods. On the strength of a social-democratic platform with a much kinder take on The Times editorial as its rallying cry, Labour easily won the election.

When Churchill passed away in 1965, there were plenty of tributes and eulogies from all sides. It felt like the end of an era, perhaps even the end of a country, observed Richard Crossman, a prominent Labour Party scholar and member of Harold Wilson's Cabinet, of his forced attendance. How mistaken he was. several others as well.

At the time, it did seem as though the post-war settlement, the slow decolonization of other countries, and the establishment of a welfare state with its cozy, happy-families vibe had put an end to the injustices of the past and provided the groundwork for a post-Churchill modernism. Edward Heath, the leader of the Conservative Party, was a fervent supporter of Europe; Wilson, the prime minister, was a more hesitant convert. Geographically speaking, Europe is little more than a cape linked to the enormous Asian continent. However, for post-war politicians, Europe would become the symbol of optimism and the center of Western civilization. With the exception of the Judeocide, its crimes both at home and abroad and its wars—imperial, civil, and religious—were all but forgotten.

The majority of the obituaries praised Churchill's leadership during the war. Opinion in the nation was significantly more divided on other topics. The propaganda intended to build morale and in which Churchill had both created and taken part spoke of group tenacity. He had displayed great rhetorical strategy in this regard. The history of that endurance was much longer and deeper than the heroic appeals of the time, which his eulogists neglected to mention.

There were still many people alive today who had been affected by the enormous unemployment in the 1920s and 1930s. Comments like "My family (or my father) hated Churchill" were frequent. When the war was almost over, many of the soldiers who had cheered him on earlier in the conflict voted against him. Then, memories lasted longer.

Churchill embodied the violent, haughty, complacent, arrogant incubator of white supremacy of the more adventurous element of the British ruling class, even when he was not actively involved. His military aristocracy background was advantageous to him, but not many people would take him seriously. After the founding duke passed away, Churchill's forebears in the dukedom of Marlborough did not produce any notable individuals outside Winston and his father, Randolph, as Roy Jenkins and others have noted. A trend, one may add, that is still going strong today. Soames is merely a supporting figure in P. G. Wodehouse.

Churchill, in contrast to many of his contemporaries, was not content with becoming a backroom boy or a submissive Member of Parliament. Above all, he was an activist for imperialism. For the cause that was always front in his mind—the British Empire—he wanted to fight, kill, and, if necessary, perish. Kill all of its adversaries, both at home and abroad. Additionally, beliefs supportive of white supremacy were easily introduced in situations where whites were obliged to slaughter other whites (Boers, Irish, Germans, and post-1917 Russians).

In Churchilliana, the boom started forty years ago. Since then, Churchill's history has subtly morphed into that of all of Britain (or at least all of England). It's simple to forget what life was like in 1965. Satirists, filmmakers, and others vehemently condemned imperial wars back then. The jeering of Joan Littlewood Oh! Stratford's Theatre Royal was filled for What a Lovely War, a vicious attack on the First World War. The cult of the Imperial Great Game was exposed in Richardson's Charge of the Light Brigade. The ascent of Margaret Thatcher, the Falklands War, and Churchill's instrumentalization, which led to his elevation to the role of a national icon thanks to Thatcher, Blair, and Johnson, would have been difficult to predict at the time. Both sides of the Atlantic have witnessed the growth of mythology.

Most of the paper shrines honoring Churchill and his conflicts, both little and large, are surrounded by an overpowering incense odor. Their effectiveness, along with that of the celluloid equivalents, cannot be disputed. But it is undeniable that a new conversation has been started thanks to the student decolonizers and their allies.

Chapter 1:
A World of Empires

Churchill wrote in his autobiography, "My Early Life," "I was a child of the Victorian era, when the structure of our country seemed firmly established, when its position in trade and on our seas was unmatched, and when the realization of the greatness of our Empire and of our duty to preserve it was ever growing stronger." When Churchill was born in 1874, Britain ruled the world as the leading empire, having a greater worldwide influence than its competitors. Although it had lost its colonies in America, it still had a foothold in Canada. The conquering of India more than made up for the American losses. According to a deal negotiated by the European powers, Africa was divided.

The majority of Europeans from all classes shared a similar perspective about their different colonies. No other could compare to the Iberian conquest and occupation of a vast continent beyond a treacherous ocean for three centuries, whatever else may be said about it. That achievement was unmatched in history. However, the majority of Churchill's biographers still hold fast to the idea that whereas some empires, like the Spanish, were brutal, even barbaric, the British Empire was more benevolent and, as a result, was more well-liked by those it colonized.

The British Empire has consequently established itself as a mainstay of the heritage sector. The Thatcher governments of the 1980s (and their Blairite successors) sought to revert anti-colonial trends in the public sphere that discounted or were harshly critical of Britain's imperial past in addition to attacking the sacred spaces of the welfare state and destroying trade union militancy. There have been numerous responses to this change. Most recently, the English historian Richard Gott's masterful study of resistance to the British

Empire in Britain largely destroyed the cosmetic version of colonization.

We must view the youthful imperialist Winston Churchill via this prism. He was a unique type of Victorian-era youngster who spent his formative years in Dublin while his grandfather served as viceroy of Ireland. He took comfort in toy soldiers and frequently told tales of his distinguished military ancestor, the first Duke of Marlborough, as a little child who had been abandoned by his parents. The young Churchill's desire to join the military was only fueled by tales of the duke's strategic brilliance on foreign battlefields, not to mention his political astuteness, starting with the Glorious Revolution.

As soon as his parents abandoned him and put him to Harrow, the maltreatment persisted. He started preparing for the military academy at Sandhurst, where admission was competitive, and found solace in the school cadet corps there. The notion did not appeal to his father, Lord Randolph Churchill, a Tory MP at the time. He preferred that his son work for Rothschild or another financial institution in the City. Winston persisted despite being intimidated and in awe of his ambitious, rash, and irritable father. After two failed tries, Winston was ultimately accepted to Sandhurst.

Jennie Jerome, his American heiress mother, was just marginally a better parent. In her absence, she liked Winston very much. She was willing to sleep with the most powerful people in the world as he grew older in order to advance his career and replenish her own wallet, which had been completely depleted when the American economy crashed and destroyed her family's money. She made her way around the SW1 squares, a procedure that started while her husband was dying of syphilis and progressed quickly after his passing. According to some tales, she even slept with the king.

Churchill's cousin Sunny, who was directly descended from the duke, was not married, thus there was a chance that he could inherit the title at one point. The duchess called for the rich cavalry in the US to launch a rescue, insisting that "it would be intolerable if that little upstart Winston ever became duke." Consuelo Vanderbilt was ultimately convinced to wed the whore Sunny. Along with the heiress, there was a $2.5 million lump sum donation and a $30,000 annuity, which helped the family's finances. Eventually, a child was born. Churchill moving to Blenheim is now impossible. Winston would have to rely on himself to succeed.

However, Winston, who had just joined the 4th Hussars at age 21, felt let down. There was no imminent British colonial war in 1895. His "all [his] money had been spent on polo ponies," and he was bored at home. What is the fastest route to distinction and the shining entrance to glory then? He started looking across the Atlantic after a few enquiries. He recalled this subsequently.

The Spanish Empire was on the verge of disintegrating. It had been working to stifle the liberation movements in the Philippines and Cuba at the same time for years. José Mart, a poet and essayist in Cuba, and José Rizal, a distinguished novelist in the Philippines, served as the political and intellectual leaders of both organizations. Mart was unfortunately killed in a military battle, and Rizal was put to death by a Spanish firing squad.

Churchill was never one to pass up a chance, and this one was ideal. He requested leave from his unit in order to join the military as an observer and personally experience a colonial conflict. His father had passed away at the beginning of the year, leaving him with a meager inheritance, so he decided to use journalism to both promote himself and make some money. In order to cover the Spanish-Cuban War for a newspaper, he applied for and was granted one. He embarked on a journey to the Caribbean via the United States with another officer.

Churchill didn't need to be overly knowledgeable about the conflict he chose. He instinctively supported the Spanish side. A simple imperial force was trying to extinguish a native insurrection in blood, and that was the only explanation.

Churchill was unable to examine, much less appreciate, the perspective of the Cuban Revolutionary Party's combatants even when he could no longer deny what was happening and realized how popular it was. He had a limited understanding of Spanish. Cuba was to them what Ireland was to the British.

Churchill, who was approaching the end of his life, listened to the woeful tales of a visiting white settler from Kenya in December 1954 as he justified the necessity of the atrocities committed against the Mau Mau revolt. Churchill was mostly concerned about how these may impact Britain's standing abroad. The Kikuyu tribe was described as "a happy, naked, and charming people" on his own 1907 visit to the African colony. However, the public would now witness "the power of a modern nation being used to kill savages," he added. It's just awful. Slaves, slaves? not barbarians. They are far more challenging to deal with since they are ideas-armed savages.

'Savages' in Cuba were also in large numbers. Generals Antonio Maceo and Maximo Gómez essentially controlled the island and besieged Havana in 1895 and 1896 as the rebels garnered greater support. Without a question, the most renowned guerrilla leader of the nineteenth century was an Afro-Cuban named Maceo. Spain and its supporters entered a state of fear. Churchill called the rebels "an undisciplined rabble" made up primarily of "colored men." He expressed concern that, should the revolution succeed, "Cuba will be a black republic," making no reference to the slaves Britain had imported to add to the population of slaves Spain had amassed over the course of the previous two centuries.

The Spanish had agreed to the abolition of slavery in Cuba in 1886, but they encouraged large-scale migration from the peninsula to the island out of terror of the whole idea of a majority-black republic. A quarter of a million Spaniards immigrated to Cuba, which at the time had a population of under two million, between 1882 and 1894. Enrique Roig, a Catalan anarchist, was among them and quickly joined forces with Mart. The influx of white immigrants was insufficient in the eyes of the Spanish. The new immigrants' literacy rates were at two-thirds. The majority were workers and peasants, with Catalans making up the majority. Many turned toward Mart and Maceo on automatic pilot.

In 1896, the Spanish were on the verge of a disastrous defeat and sent out a new Captain-General to take back control. General Valeriano Weyler was chosen because of his cruelty and was well-known in Madrid for preferring animals to people. He was a hybrid of the two. In Madrid, he had supplied funding for a boarding facility for horses where they received excellent care and oats on a regular basis. To keep the guerrillas separate from the populace in Cuba, he established a network of detention camps. The results were disastrous: not only were families split apart and women and girls forced into prostitution, but up to 50% of those in the camps perished in some Cuban towns. A total of at least 170,000 "concentrated" civilian deaths—roughly 10% of the country's population at the time—were attributed to disease and starvation.

In retaliation for the death of anarchists in Barcelona, Michele Angiolillo, an Italian anarchist living in Barcelona, assassinated the latter in June 1897. A black Puerto Rican who supported the Cuban revolution persuaded Angiolillo that Cánovas would make a better target than the Spanish monarch who had been his original aim. He suggested that the prime minister's departure would actually benefit the Cuban people and offered 500 francs as a perk. According to

Richard Gott, the "three bullets" that Angiolillo fired "did as much for the Cuban independence movement as three years of combat."9 A reformist administration that promised Cuban independence was brought about by a regime shift in Madrid. By that time, the United States had invaded the Philippines and declared war on the Spanish Empire; its armed intervention in Cuba in 1898 put an end to the Spanish-Cuban War.

The youthful explorer was eager to head straight for the continent of Africa after his return from Cuba in 1896, which had already been completely colonized by Europeans. Wars were coming, and it wouldn't take much effort to get quick career advances. Instead, his superior commanders determined he should serve in India with his unit. Churchill objected and tried to modify the judgment using his titled connections, but in vain. He was keen to join the 9th Lancers, who were headed to South Africa's Matabeleland. He wrote to his mother, "This we will discuss on Friday," adding, "But my dear Mamma you cannot think how I would like to sail in a few days to scenes of adventure and excitement -- to places where I could gain experience and benefit -- rather than to the tedious land of India, where I shall be equally out of the pleasures of peace and the chances of war."

Churchill had a complex preoccupation with India, but it wasn't irrational. The British were the only modern empire to be able to seize as much land and as many people in Asia. Due to the country's excessive population, even a partial eradication was problematic in India. Additionally, they couldn't be housed in concentration or reservation camps. But the benefits far surpassed the drawbacks.

About a month prior, he had been horrified to see 36 dead bodies that the British had hurriedly buried but that Pashtun tribesmen had uncovered and dismembered. However, this was no more degrading than the frequent violence used by the British Army. Barbarism and civilization are identical twins.

There was no news as to why the British were being attacked. The Empire had previously suffered defeat in conflicts with Afghanistan. The first came to an end in January 1842 with General Elphinstone's massive British-led force being routed. Lord Auckland, the Governor-General of India, was so shocked by the news that he suffered a stroke from which he never fully recovered. The historic Afghan bazaar from the sixteenth century and other old structures were destroyed in April of the same year by General Pollock's "Force of Retribution." After exacting their retribution, the British withdrew from Afghanistan and vowed never to try another takeover.

However, the Empire insisted on delineating a legal border between Afghanistan and India in 1893, and Sir Mortimer Durand, a civil official, was sent to carry out the task. The locals frequently disregarded the 1,640-mile border that he created to separate the Pashtun tribes. The 'wild beasts' were again in uproar over this entirely arbitrary split.

After slavery was abolished in the latter decades of the nineteenth century, the white imperialist nations looked for alternatives. If the taking of people was forbidden, then the obvious next question, according to the Empire's immaculate reasoning, was "Why not take the land?" Africa beckoned because it had given rise to ancient civilizations, given birth to humanity, and most significantly, was wealthy in resources like diamonds, minerals, and later, oil. Black Africa had been weakened by regional conflicts and tribal rivalries. The group of nations with recognizable political structures was diverse and dispersed.

The first of these was the Amharic Empire's Abyssinia, which subsequently became Ethiopia. It stood apart when European vultures split the continent. It had not yet had its independence violated. In order to start a war in 1868, the British established an imperial base at Zula, south of Massawa on the Red Sea. From there, they successfully attacked the ruler's mountain city of Magdala. After the Crimean War, Britain began testing out new weapons (in this case, Snider breech-loaders). If the British had not also managed to win over the Tigre Province's legitimate ruler, who had his own issues with the Abyssinian king, the armaments alone might not have been sufficient. Italy had also shifted its attention to the area.

Africa had been set out as a continent that could be captured by European incursions throughout the nineteenth century. There was enough for everyone, so long as the white empires did not engage in acts of unrestrained greed and turn against one another. Otto von Bismarck, the first chancellor and architect of the new German state, had this viewpoint. Germany had no colonial territories when it was united. It sought to make up ground in Africa. For this reason, in 1884–1885, Bismarck called a summit of imperialists in Berlin. Three months were involved. The only thing on the true agenda was how to partition Africa most effectively. The 'civilisation', the 'older brother' of the 'humanitarian interventions' of the late 20th and early 21st centuries, was to blame for the seizure, rape, and occupation that followed.

An unprecedented occurrence in the history of imperialism was the gift of the Congo to the Belgian King Leopold II as his personal fiefdom. Only on this occasion in contemporary times had an entire territory received official, international recognition as belonging to one particular person. The Congo maintained its exceptional status for twenty-five years. The most notorious absentee landlord in the annals of contemporary imperialism, Leopold neglected to visit his property despite the fact that Congo had become his life's interest and the source of his great wealth (he was afraid of contracting "African diseases").

Leopold pronounced himself content. He and other colonial leaders believed that strong measures were required to prevent Arab traders from abducting Africans and selling them on the black market. However, as images of the atrocities started to make their way back to Europe, there were numerous statements of outrage, most often from British writers, some of whom were relieved that these crimes were being committed by an empire other than the British.

The soldiers and settlers of Leopold massacred half the Congolese people. There were between eight and 10 million people who died; exact numbers vary. The Second World War's Judeocide, which Germany and its allies committed in the majority of Europe, was the closest comparable crime committed by a European state in terms of size and scope. In Palestine, the number of unintentional victims of that crime is still being calculated every single week.

There was opposition to the colonization of Africa. Many times, the inhabitants of the continent and their leaders retaliated. European barbarism reacted as barbarism typically does: by extortion, theft, and bribery.

The Hova kingdom in Madagascar was subdued by the French in 1896 following a protracted uprising. The French had invaded the Dahomey Kingdom four years earlier. Men and women who ruled Dahomey worked to create a nation-state with a diverse ethnic population. The celibacy female battalions that made up a significant portion of King Glele's army were criticized by travel writer Richard Burton. (The author was harsher toward the male soldiers, who were not properly equipped or trained due to any fault of their own.) However, in 1892, the same army significantly damaged the approaching French column. To the chagrin of the French, the Dahomean men and women continued guerrilla warfare in the years that followed, despite losing the battle to defend their capital. The vanquished female troops were displayed as payback in Paris in the late 1890s.

The British encountered the most difficult resistance in Somalia around the turn of the century in a region they took control of as a result of the division exercise carried out by the European powers at the Berlin conference. They came up against a political-religious figure in Mohammed Abdullah Hassan who was also a poet and a superb military tactician. In its protracted struggle against European incursion, Africa produced him as the most skilled guerilla commander.

He was known as the "Mad Mullah" by the British invaders, and he was frequently referred to as such in the British press. Like others before and after him, he became a hate figure. Churchill had referred to Britain's Pashtun adversaries in Malakand as "Mad Mullahs." How could anyone who fought the kind and considerate Empire be anything other than insane? Today, Mohammed Abdullah Hassan is acknowledged as the Somali state's founder. The fact that his wife and other women were military commanders must have astounded the occupiers.

Churchill would eventually get the chance to battle in Africa, but first, some background. A religious leader named Mohammed Ahmed bin Abdullah headed the proto-nationalists in Sudan who started to challenge foreign control in the late 1800s. Mohammed Ahmed bin Abdullah identified himself as the Mahdi, the savior, whose arrival had been promised in Shi'ite Islam. The theory itself was considered heresy by the majority of Sunnis because there could only be one Prophet.

An important development in imperialist politics was the Sudanese conflict. It was a divided Britain. W. E. Gladstone, the British prime minister, disliked war and sent General Charles Gordon, a former imperial consul in Egypt, to evacuate Egyptian and British forces from Khartoum in 1884. Gordon established himself there against his orders and was surrounded. He asserted that "God is on our side" in a correspondence with the Mahdi.

The Mahdi promised the general and his men that they would not suffer harm if they left the city in peace. Gordon turned down the offer with imperial haughtiness. Gladstone succumbed to pressure despite not being persuaded that an army should be dispatched to try to remove the general. When the Mahdi's men captured Khartoum in 1885 after the expedition's failure, Gordon was killed as a martyr.

After Gordon's rescue attempt failed, another imperial warlord, General Herbert Kitchener, gathered support for a jingoist effort to bring the Sudanese patriots back to justice with the aid of the right-wing press. Queen Victoria welcomed Kitchener, who was frequently the main guest at banquets. Kitchener later rose to fame and was occasionally applauded by the general public and veterans in the streets.

The River War of 1896–1899 broke out ten years after Gordon's passing, drawing Churchill's attention to it like a moth to a lamp. He had been keeping tabs on what was happening in Africa. His tenure of duty in India, close to the Afghan border, stood out mostly because of the novelistic Henty-style report he wrote about Malakand. His main concern right now was figuring out how to start acting right now. Kitchener consistently stood in the way of his efforts in this regard. The two men didn't disagree on any fundamental issues. They were both Empire supporters. However, celebrity served as both people's impetus. With military service in Egypt, Sudan, India, South Africa, and Australia, Kitchener had a brutal international track record. The young Churchill was just seen by him as a spoiled child.

Churchill urged his mother to secure him a position using her charm. She fell flat. Churchill made a strong suggestion that he would really want to work in Africa when he was invited to tea at Downing Street by the prime minister, Lord Salisbury, who had praised his Malakand report. Later, he requested and was granted a meeting with Sir Schomberg. Salisbury's close friend and advisor Kerr McDonnell is someone who "I had seen and met in social circles since I was a child." He continued to press his case for favoritism. The reply from Kerr McDonnell was cordial but non committal. He assured Churchill that Salisbury would try his utmost. He is really happy with you, but he will not go any farther. He could be willing to phrase the query in a way that makes it clear what he wants the outcome to be. If the response is negative, you shouldn't anticipate him pressing the issue. It was.

Churchill was not going to give up. In the end, he managed to get around Kitchener with the aid of additional family friends who worked for the War Office, and he was told that he had been "attached as a supernumerary Lieutenant to the 21st Lancers for the Soudan Campaign... report at once to the Abbasiyah Barracks, Cairo to the Regimental Headquarters." You will travel at your own expense, and no costs of any kind, should you get hurt or killed, will be covered by British army finances. He was now working as a freelance soldier and journalist.

Although he had prevailed, the conflict with Kitchener had been crippling. In My Early Years, Churchill's first and greatest autobiography, which was released in 1930, a whole chapter, self-pitying and self-justifying, is devoted to it. He had learned that "there were many ignorant and unkind people who did not view my activities favorably." With time, there would be an increase in the number of these persons. Their target accused them of acting out of envy. Churchill's own description of their remarks, however, seems to indicate differently. It was the obvious cronyism that was disliked.

Although he wasn't the only young man to take use of his social and class benefits, Churchill was the subaltern who made the most of them. Although he was angry at the abuse he received, the labels his critics gave him, like "Medal-hunter" and "Self-advertiser," seemed modest even for the period.

Churchill made an effort to see the positive side of things as he traveled from Cairo to the conflict area in Sudan. "The excellent arrangements made for our comfort and convenience," he said, "are wonderful." The breathtaking countryside over the 400-mile train ride was enjoyable, and "everyone's excitement and thoughtless gaiety with which they looked forward to the unquestionably approaching battle" also helped.

Late in the summer of 1898, Churchill arrived in Sudan. On September 2, the Battle of Omdurman took place. On the Nile, a British fleet was waiting. Faced with 15,000 Sudanese, a British Army of 25,000 troops (8,000 of them were white) was present. Given the numerical and technological disparity, a British triumph was not unexpected. Characteristic quotes from Churchill include, "It was the last link in the long chain of those spectacular conflicts whose vivid and majestic splendor has done so much to invest war with glamour," and "It was the last link in the long chain of those spectacular conflicts."

Morris, Eleanor Marx, Ernest Belfort Bax, and a few dozen other people signed a declaration issued in 1885 by the 'Provisional Council of the Socialist League' that contested the official justifications for the Sudanese war. They rightly noted that Mohammed Ahmed (the Mahdi) had indicated a willingness to discuss the systematic removal of British garrisons. Even though Wilfrid Scawen Blunt, a trusted middleman, had told the British that he could help get Gordon released, the brigands in London wanted to punish the locals. They fell short.

General Kitchener replied that he was planning to present the skull to the Royal College of Surgeons after hearing that the Queen was upset and had equated the outrage on the tomb as a deed befitting of the Middle Ages, especially since the Mahdi had been a "man of certain importance."

The best expert in this area was Kitchener. It was well known how badly he wanted to become viceroy of India. John Morley, the Liberal Cabinet's Secretary of State for India, blocked the proposal. Whatever else was needed, he was well aware that autocratic sadism was not what British India at the time needed. The monetary award given to Kitchener upon his return from Sudan was opposed by Morley and fifty other MPs despite the official junketing and media-promoted praise.

Similar to this, Churchill's entire life was driven by the necessity of maintaining, growing, and defending the British Empire, no matter the financial or moral cost. He believed that bringing civilization to the barbarians and lower peoples was beneficial for all of humanity and expressed this belief. How could they possibly lose? Gandhi is known for his famous response to the question posed by an American journalist decades later: "It would be a good idea."

Churchill took a more refined method than Kitchener, but the project remained the same. He said that the Nile Valley had now been exposed to "the civilizing influence of commercial enterprise" because of the victory at Omdurman. Kitchener was a practical technician rather than an idealist. His desire manifested itself in the shape of colonial conquest and taking a bloody bath in glory. He was more brutal than, but not significantly different from, other members of the imperial military elite in this regard. All of these things applied to Churchill as well. However, his conceit only served to increase his danger.

The last conflict of the nineteenth century on the African continent took place in South Africa between the British and the Boers, who were Huguenot refugees from France who had fled the Edict of Nantes and were descended from the Dutch who had settled in the Cape in the seventeenth century to establish an outpost for the Dutch East India Company. From that point on, the Cape Colony was affected by a power seesaw in Europe, with Britain acquiring control and the Dutch coming back; this process was repeated until British rule was unassailable.

There were, however, areas where the latter predominated due to the large number of Dutch settlers and the development of the language. An ultra-Anglophile of Dutch descent who later served as South Africa's prime minister and was close to Churchill advocated a solution in which Cecil Rhodes would take on the role of the real monarch and lead a coalition government of several European nations. The Boers showed no enthusiasm. They desired independence from London, ownership of their own mines and wealth, and self-governance.

The casus belli were gold mines in African (now Boer) territory. British officers arrived in 1899 fully prepared with valets, grooms, and hampers filled with delicacies from Fortnum & Mason (which had proudly, and absurdly, boasted since the Crimean War that it catered to soldiers and officers alike). Kitchener was once again in the lead, with Churchill playing the role of the journalist forever on his heels. The British believed they would easily win because they were haughty and overconfident in their achievements. They were caught off guard by the fact that this was not a "gentlemanly war."

The actual conflict matched the traditional British Army, which wore red tunics and pith helmets, against Boer guerrilla forces, which often consisted of 25 men or less and rode ox wagons. These Boer troops became skilled at causing trouble for British columns and eluding arrest. While it was generally acknowledged that British intelligence was subpar, the Boers were well-versed in the area. Kitchener was fortunate to come out of the war with his reputation unharmed.

The biggest number of British casualties during the war—1,200—came from his first foray. Many top commanders had their commands withdrawn. It was considered that too many of them had given up out of pure cowardice. According to Somerset Maugham, "the majority nerved themselves to a stouter courage" after "some were shot and more cashierred."15 Over 3,700 British officers perished in all. Three times as many casualties were sustained by the imperial yeomanry, which was hastily enlisted under the promise of five shillings per day. Losses brought about desperation, which brought about war crimes. At home, Liberal Party leader Henry Campbell Bannerman called the actions of the British troops "barbarous." He had great support from the Guardian, whose reporter, the liberal thinker J.A. Hobson spoke with Olive Schreiner and the leader of the Transvaal, Paul Kruger, to offer a different perspective. After an earlier "informal" attempt had failed, the scoundrel Rhodes had pushed for the start of the war. Rhodes was the one who encouraged Kitchener with financial support from South Africa. Hobson used the anti-Semitic term "Jewish financiers" to refer to businessmen, but his main goal was to investigate and conceptualize how national capitalism gave way to imperialism. This endeavor led to the creation of his iconic piece Imperialism.

Chapter 2:
Skirmishes on the Home Front

The politically engaged elements of a developing working class in Britain fought valiantly and gave their lives for them to obtain fundamental social and political rights for nearly a century (1819–1914). The owners of property and their political supporters met them with fierce opposition, supported by the church, the police, the judiciary, and, where necessary, military force. Regular political upheaval during most of the nineteenth and early twentieth centuries had contributed to the combined and unequal growth of consciousness that aided in the establishment of both the ruling class and the radical and youthful labor movements of the era. Each side kept a remembrance of the past. In one instance, optimism, in the other, worry.

In a time of political turbulence and unease among the ruling elite, Churchill entered politics in 1900 and was elected as a Conservative to the House of Commons the following year. Joseph Chamberlain, the head of the Liberal Party, had railed against the new affluent in 1885, the magnates who had amassed fortune in cities and on the seas and were busy constructing their opulent estates in the countryside. He was not against their accumulation of money, but he believed there should be a cost. In order to democratize noblesse oblige, Chamberlain raised the following query as he began his push for an early welfare state: "I ask what ransom will property pay for the security which it enjoys?" Attacked for using the word "ransom," he later changed it to the less unpleasant "insurance," but the point remained the same. The wealthy class was on edge.

The British radical century had mirrored the trajectory of the 1789–1815 French Revolution. Large crowds picketed and attacked army recruitment centers in Holborn, the City, Clerkenwell, and Shoreditch in 1794, during the height of the revolution across the Channel, eventually setting them on fire after three days of rioting. The authorities' expectation that Napoleon's loss at Waterloo and his imprisonment on Saint Helena would significantly lower the radical climate at home was only partially realized after 1815. Tom Paine's supporters congregated in various places with even more extreme currents. The development and existence of a police force, which was first constituted as a unified public entity to regulate labor on the Thames ports in 1800, was met with fierce opposition by the non-privileged classes.1 The greater powers of a centralized police force would result in "a system of tyranny; an organized army of spies and informers, for the destruction of all public liberty, and the disturbance of all private happiness," according to reformers who accepted that localized, preventive police units might be required to protect homes and businesses. Every other form of law enforcement is a result of despotism.

The radical culture of the era significantly contributed to the growth of discussion groups in the absence of political organizations. Established in 1819, Thomas Wooler's The Black Dwarf became the most widely read radical weekly. Wooler, a printer from Sheffield, was a brave editor. The satire in the magazine was occasionally over the top, but it was always done with good intentions. Wooler frequently wrote his pieces as though they were written in stone and encouraged writers to choose the expression method that felt most natural to them.

Because of Shelley's poetry, the use of cavalry bayonets against the Reformers at Peterloo is the most well-known instance of class conflict in industrializing Britain, yet the rally itself wasn't quite a bolt from the blue. It has been extensively discussed in monographs, and most recently, Mike Leigh produced an enormously educational film—a rarity these days. The Political House that Jack Built, a compilation of the scathing satires written at the time by Messrs. Hone and Cruikshank, sold something in the neighborhood of 100,000 copies. The actual number of readers should, at the absolute least, be quadrupled because most pamphlets, periodicals, etc., were shared and passed around in taverns and other gathering places. The Making of the English Working Class by Edward Thompson is still the gold standard for contextualization. His depictions of the different radical ideologies that were prevalent at the time, without which the massive gathering in Manchester would not have been conceivable, add depth to his portrayal of Peterloo.

Tens of thousands of people gathered on St. Peter's Field ('Peterloo' was a satirical term that remained) to demand the right of all men to become adult males. This may seem insignificant now, but at the time, the ruling elites, who equated even a partial democracy with revolution, viewed it as ultra-radical. There were trees, lampposts, and halters everywhere, if summary justice is required, to make examples of any hardened or incorrigible villain, or any great or small plunderer of property, mordantly advised readers of his magazine, Medusa, Or, Penny Politician. Thomas Davison, a radical bookseller in Smithfield, titled one of his editorials "The Blowing Up of the Present System." How would the few benefit if the majority had the power to vote?

Wooler continued by claiming that the state and the government had approved the use of force as well as the actions of the magistrates, who "were the cause of the slaughter" by acting illegally. He made the same connection between domestic atrocities and murder abroad as the Female Reformers. In the end, the same techniques were employed and would be maintained.6 In Amritsar, India, in Jallianwala Bagh, where tens of thousands had assembled to call for an end to colonial brutality, the British General Reginald Dyer would issue an order to his soldiers to block off the area a century after Peterloo. Women and children were present, just as they were at Peterloo. Machine guns were used by the infantry in place of sabres. They were instructed to intimidate the populace. At least 500 people were murdered and more than 1,000 were injured as a result of ongoing shooting.

The English and French revolutions can serve as models to help provide an answer. Although the latter's influence was far greater by the nineteenth century, references to "leveling" and the "good old cause" persisted in the political lexicon of radicals and later socialists. Although many of the Reformers were motivated by various currents in Methodism, French Jacobinism served as an important source of inspiration for radical movements in the nineteenth century. A month after the massacre, 300,000 people would be out in the streets of London seeking justice from all the factions, both extreme and less radical. They would later, in 1838, be more systematically united by the Chartists in the first serious effort to organize dissident forces across the nation and create an extra-parliamentary opposition movement, with the representation of the disenfranchised masses (their male section) as its primary goal in the House of Commons.

However, radicals were contemplating small-scale civil battles against the gentrified landowners well before Chartism. The most ambitious were convinced that an act of bravery may start an uprising. that is? like killing Lord Liverpool the Prime Minister and his Cabinet while they were having lunch at Lord Harrowby's residence in Grosvenor Square. Although the 1820 "Cato Street conspiracy" was thwarted, a sizable number of radical minds at the time were consumed by the vision of eliminating the entire Cabinet. They also didn't keep their terrorist intentions a big secret.

Spencer Perceval, Liverpool's predecessor at Downing Street, had been assassinated in the Commons' lobby in 1812. As a young prosecutor, Perceval assisted in the indictments of radical John Horne Tooke and religious Tom Paine. When Colonel Edward Despard (1751–1803) was prosecuted for high treason and executed by hanging, he served as the lead prosecutor. According to Perceval, Despard was preparing to kill George III and seize the Bank of England and the Tower of London.

Despard was a key figure in the Jacobin underground and came from an Irish landowning family. When Lord Nelson testified on his behalf in court, he said that Colonel Despard "could have shown more zealous attachment to his Sovereign and his Country than any man could have shown in his younger days as an officer." But all of that happened in the past. The colonel's mindset has drastically changed. His Irish heritage, his experiences in Jamaica and the Central American colonies, his marriage to Catherine, an Afro-Caribbean who actively opposed slavery, his connections to the Irish Republican Robert Emmet, and, according to some, British and Irish Jacobin groups in France had all combined to radicalize him. As a strong opponent of enclosure and supporter of Irish independence, he started collaborating with the covert United Irishmen organizations operating in England as well as the radical reform organization the London Corresponding Society. Despard wanted to build a revolutionary army that could fight for the liberation of both Britain and Ireland. He attracted a sizable number of soldiers, one of which was a Grenadier Guard whose father had given his son the name "Bonaparte." Despard's trial judge criticized him for supporting "the wild and Leveling principle of Universal Equality," and after his execution, he rose to martyrdom as a radical figure who was well regarded by the underclass.

Lord Liverpool had already abolished habeas corpus in England and Ireland before Peterloo. After that, his Parliament passed the oppressive Six Acts, which imposed strong restrictions on the right to free speech and assembly as well as harsh penalties for anybody who disobeyed the new rules. In an effort to drive out radical publications, it also levied a special tax on them. Spy agents from the Home Office were scurrying about, infiltrating one group of radicals, silently observing another, and stirring them up to commit extreme deeds in order to eliminate them forever. Others were hard at work creating false information (and leaflets) to demonize the radicals. The sooner they could be found, apprehended, and put in jail or executed, the safer it would be for the rulers, there was a real worry that certain factions could demand vengeance for the killing. A clerk magistrate declared to a prisoner in the dock a month after Peterloo: "I believe you are a downright blackguard reformer," fusing religious dogma with the impartiality of the legal system. The rope is already over some of your necks, so some of you reformers should be hanged and some of you will undoubtedly be.

Spence propagated the need for a revolution similar to the one in France and a Franco-British union to liberate the world up until the time of his death in 1814. The 'forty disciples' placed him to rest, but his spirit didn't go to sleep. Five years later, his supporters were still gathering in rooms at different bars.10 A Home Office spy said that John Thistlewood, a former soldier who was one of their number, said, "High Treason was committed against the people at Manchester." I made the decision that the perpetrators of the atrocity should pay for the sins of the innocent people they killed.

The Spenceans were given six Home Office spies. George Edwards, one of them, served as the main provocateur. He found the rooms at

1a Cato Street, off Edgware Road in the Marylebone neighborhood of London, where they plotted, and he spread the erroneous rumor that the Cabinet, including Wellington, the victor of Waterloo, had been invited to supper by Lord Harrowby, the Lord President of the Council in the government. The only topic on the agenda for the first meeting at Cato Street—which was chosen because it was close to the location of the alleged supper in Grosvenor Square—was how to assassinate Liverpool and his Cabinet as they sat down to eat. The Spenceans had a serious objective. Their goal was to start a revolution. Although one of the defendants, James Ings, shouted, "The Attorney General knew all the plans for two months before I was acquainted with them," and claimed George Edwards had suggested some of the more gruesome acts, a pro-government account based on information from the Home Office spies was presented at trial and was not denied by the defendants.

The Chartist uprising that engulfed Britain from 1832 to the early 1860s has been the subject of a lot of writing. Looking back, it is hard to argue that this was the most impressive organization the British working class had ever built. It built a close relationship between its supporters and its leaders, whatever defined, as a movement as opposed to a party. On the Charter itself, there was the only actual consensus. Although talk of extreme upheaval was always in the air, the tone now appears tame because the goal was reform rather than revolution. The Chartists had issues within their own ranks to deal with. For instance, there was early resentment toward Irish immigrants in Manchester. The two organizations were brought together under the Chartist flags by radicals on both sides. A similar trend was underway in Liverpool, a city where the slave trade had contributed to its prosperity and where Irish immigrants had initially been met with chants of "green niggers" from the inhabitants.

Despite the growing desire for dramatic reforms in the nineteenth century, few compromises were granted. The authorities of the day and Whig historians saw the constitutional aspirations of Chartism as barely short of revolution. Were their worries well-founded?

On paper, the Charter was a rather modest document. In the ensuing commotion, it is possible to forget that the language of political manifestos is frequently an extension of a central and at least potentially unifying demand. The Chartists outlined what it would entail if the majority of men were fairly represented in Parliament. They excluded any type of social or economic leveling, let alone the overthrow of the House of Lords or the monarchy, two significant accomplishments of the English Revolution in the seventeenth century. However, it shouldn't be inferred from their absences that many of the people who collectively headed the Chartists and the radical Jacobin organisations that came before them did not have similar beliefs.

Daniel M'Naghten, a Glasgow-based Scottish woodturner, made a serious attempt to assassinate Prime Minister Robert Peel four years later, in 1843. He had been following Peel for a few days, but on the intended day he confused the prime minister with his private secretary, Edward Drummond. From Charing Cross to Downing Street, he followed him, got close, and shot him. Five days later, Drummond passed away. M'Naghten's astute attorney, Alexander Cockburn, successfully claimed at his trial that he was insane at the time the crime was committed and secured his acquittal, creating a precedent for "criminal insanity" in English law.

By 1848, revolutionary forces on the Continent had intensified and swiftly quashed the Chartists' hopes for democracy. When King Louis Philippe was overthrown and the Second Republic was established in France on February 24, it immediately caused tremors across Italy, Germany, Austria/Hungary, and Bohemia. Switzerland, Denmark, Romania, Poland, and of course Ireland all felt distant echoes. While it would take years for other groups to be put down, the collapse of the sizable Chartist demonstration on Kennington Common in April effectively put a stop to any hope of a Britain-wide uprising. But once more, Chartist organizations in towns and cities saw this as a setback rather than a victory. A few decades later, trade unions, the Independent Labour Party, and subsequently the Labour Party would be founded by their political heirs. All three would eventually mirror the desires of the masses, both in part and in significant proportion.

The process of trade union creation in Britain resembled Chartist organizational structures in certain ways. It was not even, with some places being more stable than others. Early in the nineteenth century, strikes occurred in Scotland, Tyne and Wear, and London (coachmakers in 1819; compositors for The Times in 1810). On April 1st, 1820, 60,000 employees in Glasgow participated in a political general strike. Home Office agents had incited a fight between a small number of weavers and the 10th Hussars, claiming the strike was a precursor to revolt. So many precursors, so few uprisings. Ironworkers in Wales were organized by trade unionist Dick Penderyn to fight a defensive guerrilla battle against yeomanry and regular troops. In 1831, he was apprehended, put on trial, and killed. Both before and after 1819, opposition was strong in Lancashire. The first Trades Union Congress was established in this location in 1868 when trade unionists from all around the nation assembled at the Mechanics Institute. The trades of the United Kingdom should hold an annual congress, the resolution read, "that it is highly desirable, for the purpose of bringing the trades into closer alliance, and to take action in all Parliamentary matters pertaining to the general interests of the working classes." It was unanimously approved.

"Parliamentary matters" was a reference to the radical Reformers, the Liberal Party, a coalition of Whigs, a few Peelites, and the Liberal Party. The TUC resorted to the latter, if not entirely, to request and offer assistance. The TUC established the Labour Party in 1900 as a pressure group in an effort to achieve direct labor representation. In the 1906 election, which was a landslide for the Liberals due to soaring food prices, popular outrage, and a rift within the Tories, it won 29 seats.

Churchill had supported free trade all of his political career. Along with 60 other Conservatives, he had voted against the principal's renunciation by their own government. Churchill joined the Liberals after leaving the Conservatives, in contrast to the others. His coworkers never forgiven him for this 'treachery'. Because free trade was not the main point of contention between the two parties. Each stood for a particular force. The Tories (and Churchill) represented landlords, the monarchy, the church, and the extreme patriotism of the Empire. The Liberals provided a safe haven for extreme republicans and atheists, as well as support for Irish Home Rule and non-conformist religion. The majority of the political establishment accused Churchill of "self-advancement." The Tories saved their special vitriol for him when he was elected as a Liberal MP for NorthWest Manchester in 1906 and granted a cabinet position.

Churchill served as the Admiralty's first secretary before being promoted to home secretary as a Liberal member of the Cabinet. How would he perform in the domestic war? Churchill's hostility toward a working class that was frantically trying to organize itself against a brutal ruling class left a permanent stain on his political reputation, and for good reason. He was both a liberal and a conservative at the same time. He was vehemently opposed to the growth of Labourism because he saw it as a perilous alien incursion into the formerly secure realms of British politics. He feared both its expansion and that of the organized labor movement and the unemployed, who had started to defect from the Liberals and support Labour. Churchill and the top executives of the two major political parties were disturbed by this development. Both were unaware that repression would hasten the process.

Strikes, street fights, problems for mining families, mass picketing, theft of neighborhood stores, etc. all occurred in South Wales in 1910. The conservative press had given the idea that the area was the center of conflict and class struggle. Based on the potential "collapse of law and order," the newspapers ran a campaign of dread. Rarely was the fact that the mine owners' obstinacy had caused this highlighted. A total of 950 miners were locked out in September 1910. Management accused them of taking a "go-slow" on a fresh seam in the Ely Pit. The answer came right away. All of the pits in the South Wales mining cartel known as the Cambrian Combine were affected by a strike. Thousands of miners gathered in front of the sole active pit on November 7. After a series of baton charges and intense hand-to-hand combat, the constabulary was able to drive the miners back to Tonypandy Square, where the strikers and their families destroyed some storefront windows and challenged mounted police who had been urgently sent in from Cardiff. There were injuries on both teams.

Churchill became involved in what would now be considered to be a minor "terrorist episode" seven weeks after Tonypandy. Two radical Latvian Jews engaged the Metropolitan Police in combat during the Siege of Sidney Street, commonly known as the Battle of Stepney. The East End of London has long served as a refuge for people fleeing persecution in their home nations. This tradition dates back to the Huguenots. In Tsarist Russia and its Baltic holdings, terrible pogroms had been committed against Jewish asylum seekers and refugees.

The 100 Sidney Street building quickly caught fire. Churchill instructed the Fire Brigade to let it burn on his own authority. Later, two burned bodies were discovered. Churchill's presence ensured that what could have been a minor footnote in London's stormy history would never be forgotten. One of the Latvian revolutionaries, nicknamed as "Peter the Painter," is honored by a plaque in the roadway. Contrary to popular belief, Churchill's top hat was never damaged by stray fire. Simply adding "color" to his function, that was.

For an additional four years, the class struggles that were sparked in South Wales and other places persisted. The Liberal administration played soft cop, hard cop in the summer of 1911, when a dock strike in Liverpool and a potential nationwide rail strike were both in the offing. The chancellor, Lloyd George, and Churchill took on the roles of the two officers. The former, through his unrivaled demagogy, proposed reforms; the latter, through conviction, issued threats and made no effort to hide his intentions to go to war. He only required a wire from George V for assistance. The king urged people to discard all caution at this time, saying that reports from Liverpool indicated that the situation there was more akin to a revolution than a strike. The Mersey needed soldiers and a warship to be moored, according to the Lord Mayors of Birkenhead and Liverpool. Churchill complied with both demands.

Churchill ordered troops to be maintained ready for action because a railway strike was imminent; as a result, Manchester Railway Station and London's Hyde Park seemed to be armed camps. The Manchester Guardian's founding editor, C. P. Scott, parted with Churchill, whom he had previously backed, because this proved to be a step too far. Churchill, a Liberal home secretary, and the newspaper had a difficult but necessary disagreement. Any one politician's hunger for war had to be put behind the interests of the Liberal Party and the government.

Churchill embraced a portion of the reformist agenda, but his passions lay elsewhere. It is practically certain that a continuation of the railway strike would have produced a swift and certain degeneration of all the means, of all the structure, social, and economic systems in that great quadrilateral of industrialism, from Liverpool and Manchester on the west to Hull and Grimsby on the east, from Newcastle down to Birmingham and Coventry in the south. Although disgusting, this was partially grounded in reality. The ruling class was challenged by a growing working class. Churchill had always found solace in violence.

Chapter 3:
The 'Great' War

Imperial avarice was the main factor that led to the conflict. Given that they owned or controlled most colonies and economic powerhouses worldwide, the British elite was unable to stay out of the war. They were unwilling to cooperate with the Germans in any way. With the exception of the Ottoman and the Japanese, all of the engaged empires had their main administrative centers in Europe. The world had been divided into colonies, which the European nation-states had dominated. The two latecomers to nation-statedom, Germany and Italy, were eager to compete for a greater piece of the earth within the pack of wolves.

Three important individuals were part of the Liberal government in Britain under Asquith: Sir Edward Grey, at the Foreign Ministry, Winston Churchill, at the Exchequer, and Lloyd George, at the

Exchequer. After the 1906 election, the Liberals implemented social welfare measures, which Churchill had championed. During the 1911 constitutional crisis, when the House of Lords attempted to stop the reforms with the support of the king, Churchill also stood behind Lloyd George. Prior to two years ago, he had sided with Lloyd George in dismissing the naval estimates before quickly retracting his position. A German navy ship's stop in the Moroccan port of Agadir in July 1911 served as a signal for what was becoming increasingly obvious to everyone. Berlin wanted to antagonize and criticize the French for sending troops into the Arab state's interior. The German commanders were requesting some land for their own budding empire, not opposing French expansionism.

Although there were no direct British investments in the Maghreb, a burgeoning commercial and naval competition with Germany was raising questions. In addition, Britain was resolved to thwart any attempts by Germany to conduct business with any of its numerous colonies and semi-colonies around the world. Despite this, the Germans continued to expand their own geographical control by making incursions into the Ottoman Empire, the Balkans, and south-eastern Europe. The enormous iron riches in France and the enormous coal deposits in Germany's Ruhr Valley served as symbols of the industrial rivalry between France and Germany. It was the desire of manufacturers and the politicians they supported on both sides to combine coal and iron. British sympathies were with the French on this issue.

The crises that marred the five years leading up to the start of the First World War in 1914 were brought on by these rivalry. There were already lender and borrower states throughout the world. Through a combination of direct and semi-direct colonies, the British were able to preserve their dominion in Africa and Asia. The British naval served as the last-resort bailiff in cases where loans had been granted, including to China, Egypt, and Argentina. However, British trade required ongoing access to those nations. All of this would eventually be contested if Germany were to emerge as the dominating force in Europe.

Churchill was the ultimate political exponent when it came to prioritizing British interests, whether he was in or out of office, sitting on the Liberal front bench or a Tory berth. And the threat of oncoming war fueled his zeal. Churchill, his longtime ally Viscount Haldane at the War Office, and Foreign Secretary Edward Grey were committed to war. They had the covert Asquith and the less combative Lloyd George on their side. The statement "the lights are going out all over Europe" is attributed to Grey, who was both a lamp-snuffer and a frothing imperialist. Although they never got along personally, Churchill was certain of his position on what Britain should do next.

In his insightful history of Britain in July 1914, released on the centennial, Douglas Newton revealed the breadth of the divisions inside Asquith's Cabinet. If the administration blindly committed itself to providing guarantees to its Entente friends, cabinet members in favor of some form of neutrality threatened to go public and leave. On July 27, colonial secretary Lewis Harcourt bragged that eleven out of the government's nineteen members shared this opinion, forming a "Peace Party" that, if necessary, would dissolve the Cabinet in the interest of our abstention.

It is a tale of deceit and making decisions in advance. For instance, on July 26, Churchill issued a "stand-fast order" to the navy, publicized it to the media the next morning, and handed the Cabinet a predetermined outcome. Once more acting without consulting the Cabinet out of concern that they may interpret his order as "a provocative action," he ordered the Royal Navy to battle stations.

Theobald von Bethmann Hollweg, a top counsel to the Kaiser and a very bright civil servant from a family of intellectuals, proposed giving Britain advantages in exchange for maintaining its neutrality. In exchange for Britain remaining neutral and France losing the war, the Germans agreed not to acquire any more land in Europe. Germany would seize control of all French overseas territories, but Belgium would remain unaffected. Asquith and Grey flatly declined the offer since they saw no reason to bother the Cabinet over such a trifling matter. There was nothing left to say other than that the offer was "dishonorable."

After a fun supper at Downing Street that same evening with Asquith and the Tsar's ambassador, Churchill fully activated the navy reserves, making it clear that Britain was getting ready for war. At the dinner, Asquith gave a "complicit" glance that was correctly interpreted as approval. This went against a prior Cabinet resolution to forbid such action. But why should a parliamentary democracy deal with the ministers or Parliament when the monarch and prime minister are both vehemently in favor of war? Numerous articles have been written regarding how the German ruling class' exclusivity led to a degree of institutional rigidity in the nation's political system. This was true, but the British system, despite appearing more flexible, was nevertheless run by a group that made important decisions without consulting the House of Commons, the purported source of democratic political authority.

The German Social Democratic Party (SPD) was established in 1875, four years after Bismarck had approved full male suffrage. In Britain, the Labour Party was established in 1900, although unrestricted adult male suffrage was not granted until 1918. The German SPD had somewhat more than a million members by 1914. For several decades following the "Great War," the majority of workers would still support the Liberal or Conservative parties because Labour had not yet achieved popular appeal.6 With 110 members in the Reichstag, the SPD was already the largest party in Germany by 1890. Due to these achievements, the SPD model, its propaganda, and its leaders—in particular, Karl Kautsky and August Bebel—were loved across the Continent, including by both wings of Russian social democracy. From these progressive achievements, Britain was cut off.

Britain and France alone suffered a million casualties over the first four months of the conflict. Are there no other options besides sending our forces to eat barbed wire in Flanders, as Churchill demanded of Asquith in response to the deadlock in the trenches? When he received no adequate response, Churchill started to daydream. His goal to be the best in military strategy was well known, and the military aristocracy either openly derided him or regarded him with courteous condescension. He now recognized the impossibility of his earlier plan to invade and seize Germany via a naval attack from the Baltic Sea, but he had a new strategy. He started pleading with his Cabinet colleagues for a drive several hundred miles to the east under navy command.

This strategy was under consideration before the Ottomans decided to join the Central Powers. The revised version sounded better since it was embellished with Churchillian flourishes. Map victories are as erratic as laughs in the dressing room before a performance. Military chiefs did not entirely support the plan, but the Cabinet did. The first shots would be aimed at Gallipoli. Churchill was fully aware that "the price to be paid in taking Gallipoli would no doubt be heavy," but he insisted that the benefits would surpass the costs in terms of lives lost. The 'Turkish menace' could be defeated, in his perspective, with the help of 50,000 soldiers and his beloved sea lions.

Admiral Sackville Carden, the top operational commander, experienced a nervous breakdown in response to Churchill's unreasonable persistence. The passage of British and French battleships through the straits took a month. Three ships were sunk and five more were damaged by Ottoman mines. Currently, half of the fleet is inoperable. The person who took over for Carden didn't ask London for permission. He informed Churchill that he would wait for military reinforcements and then issued an order for a departure. Any benefit that had been envisioned was now unachievable.

A full month later, when the troops finally did arrive, they were surrounded on the beaches and made up disproportionately of cannon fodder from Australia and New Zealand mobilized in the ANZAC. The Ottoman forces engaged in severe combat because the Turkish Army had used the previous four weeks to build a nearly impregnable defense. Serious losses were incurred by the Entente, totaling 45,000 troops. There were about 2,000 Indians and almost 10,000 ANZACs. Turkish estimates were higher: 65,000 bodies needed to be buried. Yet in January 1916, the Entente eventually withdrew.

Churchill's only significant wartime undertaking, the Battle of Gallipoli, was a humiliating failure that will never be forgotten. It showed that choosing new battlefronts in order to avoid the barbed wire in Flanders did not work either. A loss of this magnitude required heads to roll. Before establishing a coalition government, the Tories insisted that Churchill be fired. Asquith was replaced by Lloyd George.

If the Ottoman Empire were ultimately defeated, the Western countries, who would divide up the Middle East, would have access to its possessions. However, the emergence of nationalism undermined conventional forms of government in the Islamic world. Mustafa Kemal (Ataturk) was the successful Turkish military commander at Gallipoli. Unlike Churchill, he gained political notoriety during that conflict, and he later played a key role in shaping post-war and post-Ottoman Turkey by enacting modernist reforms that advanced the new nation on a number of fronts. The Turkish nationalists gained confidence from their victories. The status of Istanbul was not negotiable, and if the Entente were tempted to do something foolish, they should keep Gallipoli in mind, they would make this very plain during post-war conversations.

Wherever they were still gathered, soldiers complained about the numerous delays that followed pledges of quick demobilization. Colonial forces had been sent back to the colonies, and British troops had been sent to the Middle East and Russia, respectively. The men were furious, having been beaten and at least somewhat traumatized by their experiences on the front or by the "Spanish flu," which began in 1916 and ultimately claimed 50 million lives worldwide despite being first diagnosed as a "minor infection." They insisted on better living circumstances or rapid demobilization and focused mostly on economic demands.

Churchill was fully aware that if the situation wasn't handled quickly, the atmosphere might turn more political and even insurrectionary. After all, the men involved had been trained to kill and use weapons. The majority of the soldiers were laborers who were desperately needed in the factories and mines back home. Large numbers of miners were the first to be demobbed; they would later move between conflict zones.

Soldiers at Folkestone and Dover's post-war encampments openly disobeyed military command as they marched through the cities while chanting crude but potent anti-war and anti-officer songs as they did so. Following the industrialized carnage on the Western Front, a strong pacifist sentiment had taken hold in Britain. The soldiers felt considerably more uneasy abroad. The Daily Herald's campaign to resolve complaints, run by the Soldiers, Sailors and Airmens' Union, had a particularly powerful impact on British troops stationed in Egypt and Palestine.

Six months after the Armistice was signed in France, in May 1919, excerpts from the official documents show that General Allenby had begged Churchill to "allow every pledge to be fulfilled by the War Office as there is a dangerous and growing unrest." A few days later, we warn the War Office that the reinforcements they are sending for Supply, HT, and MT are wholly insufficient, and that at the rate they are sending them, it will take a year to demob them—at which point a serious situation will develop.

There was an open rebellion at Poona in the autumn of 1919. For many soldiers, including those who were too afraid to participate in the action, Sgt. Bowker, an eloquent and radical NCO, rose to the status of a hero. In order to negotiate with the rank-and-file committees of the camp's various sections, a delegation of senior commanders was swiftly put together.

Bowker was charged with numerous, serious crimes. Officers were given instructions to appeal to the British soldiers' sense of imperial loyalty and persuade them to avoid interaction with their non-white colleagues. Churchill made concessions because he was concerned that the mutinies may extend to Indian soldiers. They did this.

Lenin stated in 1919 that "the British government is the purest form of the executive Committee of the bourgeoisie." The politician whose life and career would be enhanced by wars of all kinds would always follow Bismarck's 1862 motto in extremis: "Not by speeches and the will of the majority are the great questions of the time decided... but by blood and iron," he could have added.

Chapter 4:
The Irish Dimension

Churchill was born at Blenheim Palace in Oxfordshire, but when he was three years old, his family relocated to Phoenix Park in Dublin. In 1877, Benjamin Disraeli named John Churchill, the seventh Duke of Marlborough, as Lord Lieutenant in Ireland. Disraeli appointed his father, Lord Randolph Churchill, who had served as a Woodstock MP since 1873, as his private secretary. Winston's first voyage aboard left a lasting impression.

Disraeli and the Tories lost the general election of 1880 to the Liberals. But the unrest in Ireland only got worse. In response to the Land League's (headed by Charles Stewart Parnell) agitation, Lord Randolph, who had previously supported expanding the Irish franchise, changed his mind, sided with the landlords, and denounced Gladstone's 1881 Land Act as "communist." In actuality, the moderate reform of the Liberal prime minister (which decreased Irish rents by 20%) was accompanied by a wave of violent repression, which resulted in the arrest of over 1,000 Land League members, including Parnell.

Unionist, pro-Empire historians have romanticized the Churchill family's engagement in Ireland (with Lord Bew coming in last), as though their stay at Phoenix Park gave them a unique and sympathetic grasp of the needs and demands of the colony. This raises doubts. Just before the First World War broke out, when Churchill was a member of the Liberal government, important conferences were held to discuss Home Rule but were purposefully not minuted, implying murky dealings that needed to be kept off the record. In his own day, Lord Randolph had championed the Ulster Unionists in their adamant opposition to home rule and inspired Ulster to fight by supporting a permanent Protestant base for the Empire.

The rumors of a mutiny in the army barracks at Curragh, where 58 officers had said they would not accept Home Rule and vowed to retire rather than be forced to impose it onto Irish Unionists, alarmed him on the eve of World War One. The facts surrounding this time period and Irish nationalism in general have been hotly debated, and during Margaret Thatcher's premiership, a disagreement among Irish historians broke out. Before going back to Churchill's part, it is necessary to give a brief overview of that discussion.

The historical discussions have persisted. A calm, deliberate, and painstakingly studied challenge to England-based revisionism has been undertaken by two Irish historians, Ronan Fanning and Diarmaid Ferriter. This challenge should (but probably won't) end the matter. Their publications, Fatal Path: British Government and the Irish Revolution 1910–1922 and A Nation and Not a Rabble: The Irish Revolution 1913–1923, are damning refutations without any sign of arrogance or bombast.

Fanning, who follows British policy towards Ireland from the Home Rule crisis of the late nineteenth century to the partition of Ireland in the early twenty-first, has finally gathered all the evidence in support of this. Irish nationalists had been waiting for Home Rule, a promise made by Gladstone but never fulfilled, for twenty years. They would eventually be obliged to take a different course due to their frustration with British democracy.

The United Irishmen made contact with the French Revolutionary Army within a short period of time. Tone persuaded the French that Ireland, once liberated from the British, may emerge as a new symbol of liberty in Europe and, more importantly, a potent base against the British Empire. In order to aid the rebels in defeating the British, the French agreed to dispatch a fleet and an expeditionary force.

The battle was over five months after Vinegar Hill. Due to his refusal to seek exile in France, Wolfe Tone was kidnapped during a naval battle and taken to Dublin, where he was tried by a court martial and died under questionable circumstances on the eve of his execution. He was laid to rest in the prison cemetery. Even today, on the anniversary of his birth, the Irish republican organization has assemblies at his tomb to remember his legacy.

In the second half of the century, attention turned to parliamentary battles for Home Rule after the armed insurrection was crushed and Ireland was forcibly incorporated into the United Kingdom in 1801. Charles Stewart Parnell succeeded Wolfe Tone in this area. As the head of the Irish Parliamentary Party at Westminster and a fellow Protestant, Parnell earned the moniker "the uncrowned king of Ireland." Regarding the objective of Irish liberation, he made no concessions and was willing to take whatever measure to oust the colonizers. Both sides in the fight did not rule out the prospect of a second uprising a few decades before the First World War broke out.

The British administration put off granting Ireland home rule until after the start of World War One. Numerous unionists enlisted to fight. Less united were the nationalists. Like Gandhi on a different continent, John Redmond, the head of the collaborationist Irish Parliamentary Party, served as a recruiter for the war. 200,000 Irishmen enlisted in all. The famous quote from Redmond reads, "The government may withdraw every single soldier from Ireland and trust that her armed sons will defend the coast of Ireland from foreign invasion."

In his book Churchill and Ireland, Paul Bew describes how comforted Foreign Minister Edward Grey had felt following their encounter, allaying concerns in the House of Commons: "One thing I would say, the one bright spot in the very dreadful situation is Ireland." The situation in Ireland is not one of the factors we currently need to take into consideration. When neocon Bew writes, "Carson saw tears trickling down the cheeks of Winston Churchill as Grey spoke," one can almost picture him wiping away a tear himself. As they moved past the Speaker's chair, Carson approached him and gave him a silent handshake. Both men, together with a large number of others, could now continue the killings in Europe.

A group of committed Irish men and women, weary of years of public and individual complaints, planned to begin an insurrection with the goal of achieving Irish independence by taking advantage of Britain's engagement in the war. The Irish republic is entitled to, and hereby claims, the allegiance of every Irishman and Irishwoman, they proclaimed, "Irishmen and Irishwomen in the name of God and of the dead generations from which she receives her old tradition of nationhood."

Undoubtedly, a defeat was the result. But a setback of this size may have one of two outcomes. For decades, they can leave a community gloomy, demoralized, and politically indifferent; alternatively, within a few years, they might incite anger, resentment, a determination to undo what has been done, and readiness for further conflict. In this instance, the latter occurred, deeply impacting Irish awareness. The fact that the Irish Volunteers' commanders abruptly withdrew them from the rebellion after they had vowed to participate was hardly a secret. The little Irish Citizens Army and its allies nevertheless engaged in battle. Dublin saw violent street fights. The execution of the well-known leaders and Roger Casement's capture and execution for high treason stunned the populace in the aftermath and for years to come.

Following the Easter events of 1916, neither Churchill nor the war cabinet appreciated the scope and nature of the new Irish republicanism. They were unable to understand that the Irish revolution was a struggle for independence and a breaking away from the British crown and state, not the work of "thugs and fanatics." The philosophy behind British colonial strategy was frequently expressed as "nip the bad guys in the bud and everything will be fine." This showed that people's roles had been overly determined. Hence, in 1916, the Irish leaders were put to death. However, what was taking place in Ireland was a part of a radicalization that was occurring both during and after the First World War and that would soon spread throughout the vanquished empires and colonies.

The British government supported the formation of an Ulster Protestant equivalent as the Irish Volunteers evolved into the IRA.
After switching parties in 1908 due to disagreements over tariff reform, he was a bit more pragmatic by this time. He had to stand for reelection in his Manchester North West seat since he had been assigned to a position in Asquith's Cabinet. He informed his voters that "My opinion on the Irish question has ripened during the last two years" in light of the strength of the local Irish vote. As a result

of receiving a new education from "the inner councils of liberalism," he "became convinced that a national settlement of the Irish difficulty on broad and generous lines is indispensable to any harmonious conception of liberalism... the Liberal Party should claim full authority and a free hand to deal with the problem of Irish self-government."

It was neither the first nor the last time that imperialist leaders have attributed a population's political tenacity and stubbornness to its faith. The Church's role in shaping Irish nationalism's post-Parnell identity was the basis for Churchill and Lloyd George's hatred of Catholicism. Catholic peasants had endured centuries of brutality, starvation, and expulsion. They wouldn't give up their identities.

In Ireland, a parallel power structure was effectively established with the IRA's creation. The number of encounters between British soldiers and police forces and IRA insurgents increased. After being demoted during the Dardanelles tragedy, Churchill recovered and served as Secretary of State for War during the Irish War of Independence (1919–1921). He made a choice that, like the previous bloodbath, would only give his enemies more ammunition. He dispatched the notorious "Black and Tans" on March 25, 1920. These paramilitaries were part of the Royal Irish Constabulary (RIC), and they were used as a killing squad and a torture apparatus.

A few months prior, in October 1919, Churchill had harshly criticized the IRA. It was "a gang of squalid murderers," a gang of thieves who had evaded capture up to this point. He gave the police and soldiers who had to battle adversaries "who could not be easily identified because they could blend into the population without a trace" the highest compliment possible, which has always been a challenge for imperial nations dealing with popular opposition. The fact that hunger strikers "might get out of prison simply for refusing to take their food" really incensed him. There could be only one reply: "England must do what it takes to 'break up this murder gang'." Before long, he was discussing a shortened version of Irish independence with IRA leader Michael Collins across from him.

A copy of Smyth's speech was given by one of the officers present to Michael Collins, who forwarded it to Irish Republican Brotherhoods all around the country. Collins' own reaction? Justice must be served quickly. Smyth's tenure was under a month. On July 17, 1920, an IRA unit invaded the smoking area of an Anglo-Irish club in Cork while he was there. "Colonel, weren't you ordered to shoot on sight?" Dan O'Donovan asked as he met his eyes. Now that you are in view, get ready. Smyth was put to death right away. In Sligo, Corporal Mee enlisted in the IRA.

The United Irishmen's uprising brought tensions to a new high. In response to an IRA ambush, the paramilitaries set fire to Cork in December of that same year, resulting in extensive damage (estimated at £2 million) and the loss of 2,000 jobs.

And that was that. The IRA developed their skills in covert guerilla warfare. According to Diarmaid Ferriter, "What cannot be disputed was the formidable achievement of Michael Collins, a masterful organizer, in cultivating contacts throughout the government, but also turning some of the opposing players against their own side, and in killing detectives and intelligence officers and their agents to protect his own intelligence network."

Collins accurately noted that the stipulations set forth by the colonial power contained the compromise. It was an unheard-of thing for a soldier who had fought in the field to be chosen to conduct negotiations, he snarled angrily to a comrade. De Valera was in charge of it, not him. Of course, this was the situation. Even during division, there was a compelling case to separate two or three counties with a preponderance of Catholics from the Orange statelet. Those counties ought to have had the option to vote in a referendum, at the absolute least.

The Irish delegation, however, was not very interested in the finer points of the split, except from requesting that Ulster be included in an all-Union parliament. On the other hand, Churchill and Lloyd George had already decided in 1911 that there could be no home rule without a split. As the meeting continued, Lloyd George resorted to magic: "The theatricality and melodrama of Lloyd George's behavior

- his affected rage, his waving of papers in the air, his threats of war, his talk of Belfast deadlines and of trains and destroyers - occasioned much subsequent but essentially meaningless debate on whether he was bluffing." Whether it was a bluff or not, the British laughed quietly. They received their desired outcome since it had worked. Churchill believed that everything would be OK going forward.

The Wet Canteen, so named for its generous mixing of human perspiration and beer, was where five troops stationed at Jullundur in the Punjab on the evening of June 27th 1920 gathered. One of the soldiers had personally witnessed the savagery of the Tans. (In the cities of the Punjab, the temperature at that time of the year averaged 100 degrees Fahrenheit.) In the evening, old newspapers and letters from Ireland were distributed in the canteen. It was a social media platform where opposing viewpoints were whispered.

After the convention in London in 1921, Collins returned to Dublin with little hope. He was aware that by unwillingly signing the contract, he had sealed both his own and countless other people's fates. The treaty split Ireland in two. Sinn Féin had divisions. The Irish Free State was established when the Dáil passed the treaty by a vote of 64 to 57 following a contentious discussion. It had a slim majority because of De Valera's choice to oppose the treaty.

Collins, who was familiar with his companions, foresaw disaster. The British sent the Free Staters weapons and ammunition as the civil war broke out. Collins was murdered. The Free State government carried out numerous extrajudicial killings in addition to executing 77 republican prisoners (more than the British did after 1916). The Irish conservative thinking and the Church both wanted a strong administration in place because the War of Independence had coincided with labor and land unrest. They received one.

De Valera undoubtedly believed that his presence would promote unity in the very near future among the anti-treaty republicans because he was concerned that if they were left without a leader, they may stray too far from the movement's initial goals. However, the civil war had a long-lasting impact on republican politics.

However, the partition, which was pushed through by Bonar Law and Lloyd George and supported by Churchill père and son, continues to destabilize Irish politics. By the time 'The Troubles' broke out once more in the late 1960s, Churchill had passed away. Speaking with friends in his later years, he voiced sorrow for several imperial missteps. Not among them were the divisions that his cherished Empire imposed on three continents. The British establishment was deeply rife with outdated prejudices. If Brexit resulted in a voluntarily united Ireland, it would be a nice irony.

Chapter 5:
The Wind That Shook the World

1917 saw the start of the February Revolution in Petrograd. Over two years had passed since the start of the First World War. The terrible stalemate on the Western Front was contrasted with the German-led alliance's superior position on the Eastern Front, which would be bolstered by the Russian Revolution. A truce and a negotiated settlement had up until this moment seemed to be the only viable choice, barring the fall of one of the empires or American involvement in the conflict. Tsarist Russia was always the weakest link in the chain of Entente states. On paper, its military might looked daunting, but in 1905, the Japanese had already decimated the Tsarist navy and army, sparking uprisings in Moscow and St. Petersburg.

Churchill had grossly miscalculated the Tsarist state's vulnerabilities, while the Russian revolutionaries had greater foresight. They saw that the Tsarist social structure contained Europe's most combustible concentration of contradictions. The Stolypin dictatorship momentarily preserved its feudal state infrastructure in 1905, when it was on the verge of disintegrating. But even this regime, which is still highly praised in Russian universities today, was unable to expand the basis of a formation whose ideological underpinnings were three fundamental ideas: "Autocracy, Orthodoxy, and Nationality." In other words, the Great Russian Chauvinist movement, the Russian Orthodox clergy, and the Romanov dynasty.

The uprising of 1905 was a significant precursor to what might come. In terms of political innovation, the spontaneous formation of soviets—elected local parliaments where workers, peasants, and soldiers choose their own members—challenged the unrepresentative Duma and resulted in a brief dual power structure. Georgia and Latvia had the most violent rural uprisings. There was a political eruption caused by the combination of social and national persecution that lasted longer than anything in the city, where the army had to be dispatched to put an end to the uprisings.

Russian absolutism was put to death by the First World War. The Tsarist army had been the government's final reliable defense. The war forced enormous peasant conscription, endangering the professional army's reputation for dependability. But no Russian Army - another issue Churchill missed - could have stood up to the Imperial German Army. Germany had the greatest trained and equipped fighting force in Europe in 1914, as even France and Britain, whose own armies were bloated with colonial men, were about to learn.

The little-discussed Eastern Front was disastrous from the start. Early in the conflict, Tannenberg decisively defeated the Russian push into the Masurian Lakes. The Germans made a persistent push throughout the course of the following year, capturing Poland and Byelorussia while suffering severe losses. The frantic offensives of Brusilov in 1916 brought to some initial territorial gains, but these were reversed by Ludendorff's well-planned counteroffensive, which culminated in the worst single bloodbath of the war. Army units under the Tsar fell apart. The fatality rates are enlightening. Russia lost 2.7 million troops in three years of fighting, more than any other combatant had lost in four.

Although many other circumstances contributed to the Tsarist regime's downfall, the world war accelerated it. The Russian countryside was plagued by starvation. The 1916 crop failures were caused by a lack of labor on the land. Alarmed by the turn of events, the feckless but violent Russian bourgeoisie banded together with a moderate group of aristocrats and accused the Tsarist court of being "pro-German." The parlors of the hopeless nobles were filled with open discussion about conspiracies. A military coup was used to overthrow the Tsar as their remedy. They were supported in this by similarly desperate Allies in Petrograd. The breaking point for all of Tsarist Russia's societal contradictions had been reached. According to Lenin, the war served as the final act's potent "stage manager." 'Land, Bread, Peace' was his own brilliant slogan for the Bolsheviks, and it was a direct response to the crisis.

Churchill had been obsessed with his own career in February 1917. He was in the political wilderness following the Gallipoli disaster and focused all of his political efforts on obtaining a new Cabinet position. By April, he had reached maximum alert and was daydreaming about how he alone could restore the Tsar to the throne. He accurately realized that a victory for Lenin's Bolsheviks would endanger stability not only abroad but also at home. It would strengthen native uprisings, which would weaken the British Empire. He had to deal with very serious Conservative opposition to the idea of his re-entry while pleading with Lloyd George nonstop to let him back into the administration. As Curzon pointed out, while "he is a potential danger in opposition, in our opinion of all of us, he will as a member of the Govt be an active danger in our midst." It will be an appointment "immensely unpopular with many of your chief colleagues."

The main concern for Churchill and the Entente nations at this point was to support a Russian government that could carry on the war. Germany had to win on the Western Front if they were to win on the Eastern Front. Given the impasse on the Western front, there was another instance in which the leaders of Britain and France ought to have suggested a cease-fire. National chauvinism has lost its appeal after igniting a fervor among the populace in August 1914. A generation was being devastated as many soldiers were dying. In the military, there were a few small mutinies and desertions.

There was a revolution brewing across all of Europe. Workers and soldiers have exposed the warmongers' pretenses. Daily casualties were increasing, and morale, particularly in the French Army, had fallen due to the pain of Verdun and the Somme in 1916. Several mutinies followed. Although they were being concealed at the time, soldiers and officers on both sides were aware of what was taking place (not unlike the US GI uprisings against their superiors in Vietnam half a century later). At one point, replacement divisions had refused to be deployed to the front, and half of the French Army had openly defied its high leadership.

Panic had been brought on by the February 1917 Revolution in Washington. Though it had been seriously considered for some years, the Petrograd events made the US entrance into the war unavoidable. It was never more than shown when President

Woodrow Wilson delivered his religious homilies on "liberty and justice and the principles of humanity." Wilson removed the mask in a letter to a close friend in July 1917, writing: "By all means, England and France do not share our views on peace. They will, among other things, be financially in our hands by the time the conflict is complete, and we can then force them to adopt our way of thinking.

In April 1917, the United States formally declared war on Russia and established a special intelligence advisory council to monitor the situation. One of its members was Allen Dulles, who would later serve as the CIA's first director and, along with his brother John Foster Dulles, effectively manage the Cold War throughout the 1950s.

Armed police officers and vigilantes detained men in their homes and off the streets in July. They then 'deported' some 1,200 Bisbee mine workers and dumped them in the desert of New Mexico. Most were immigrants, many of them were from Mexico and southern Europe. They were herded into cattle vehicles and driven for sixteen hours while having weapons aimed at their heads. As in the present, parents and children were divided. Harry Wheeler, the sheriff of Cochise County, and Walter Douglas, the general manager of Phelps Dodge, the largest mining firm in the region that also controlled numerous Bisbee enterprises, including the newspaper, were responsible for the conception and execution of the plan. 2,200 workers, including pro-company miners, had been discreetly enlisted in a Loyalty League by the two.

Wilson's domestic policy showed that the name "democracy" was only a euphemism for "counter-revolution." The Palmer Raids, which started in 1919 in the midst of a post-war strike wave, resulted in the arrest, detention, and deportation of thousands of people, including anarchists, immigrants (particularly Italians, Eastern Europeans, and Jews), and suspected "Reds" by any other name. The nation's first Red Scare, an initiative of the attorney general and the Labor Department, depended on investigations by a new Justice Department agency, led by a young and aspirational J. Edgar Hoover. Immigrants were portrayed as symbols of social danger as a result of the fusion of radicalism fear and a more libertarian nativism. Two Italian workers with anarchist sympathies, Nicola Sacco and Bartolomeo Vanzetti, were wrongly charged with murder, set up by a compliant court, and electrocuted. This incident would go on to become a cause célèbre for the left in the 1920s. Step out of line, and you might not make it. Wilson's declarations that the United States will emerge "on those grand heights where the light of the justice of God shines unobstructed" sounded like the blarney they were.

Europe was in uprising, in contrast to the United States, where the left was disorganized and the 1917 revolutions' impact was therefore constrained. The Petrogradian thunderbolt electrified Germany. In Kiel, sailors staged a coup, troops defied orders, and the Kaiser was abruptly removed from power in 1918. There was a radicalization happening. Berlin has a turbulent political climate.

On the left, there was a power struggle between three working-class parties. The most significant of these, the German Communist Party (KPD), had been in development for some time when it was created by the three most influential figures on the German left: Rosa Luxemburg, Karl Liebknecht, and Leo Jogiches. Long before Lenin, Luxemburg had recognized that the German Social Democratic Party, which dominated the Socialist International, had a bad streak. Her disagreement with Karl Kautsky began in 1910–1911, when the right wing of the SPD openly endorsed Germany's display of imperial hegemony by sending the battleship Panther to Agadir.

At a public event organized by the Independents in Berlin, she continued to make the case that debating the virtues of socialism in parliament with "Junkers and bourgeois" was a waste of time. She proclaimed, "Socialism does not entail sitting in a parliament and passing laws." "Socialism means for us the overthrow of the ruling classes with all the brutality [loud laughter] that the proletariat can employ in its struggle," the speaker said.

The rage overflowed the boundaries of politics. The vicious caricature by George Grosz from April 1919, which appeared in the satirical magazine Die Pleite, conveyed much more than just leftist suffering. Many people in the nation who did not identify with the KPD or the USPD began to feel uneasy.

Even though the 1919 events in Berlin were devastating, political dissent was not completely extinguished. The harsh polarization in the country was accelerated by the penalty meted out to the vanquished Germans at Versailles, followed by the economic catastrophe of the late 1920s. The liberal ruling class struggled to reconcile conflicting interests during the Weimar Republic (1918–1933). Both the power of the revolutionary forces and the counter-revolutionary fervor of fascism and conservatism could not be tamed. A fresh internal and external conflict was being set up. The following chapter will take place in Germany again.

Once more, Churchill's animosity was motivated less by his love of the monarchy than by what he saw as a threat to the British Empire. The US's calculations had nothing to do with a love of democracy either. The new regime would have likely been made up of a lethal mixture of monarchists, liberals, conservatives, and the fascists of the Black Hundred, experts in pogroms, whose members were the most vicious elements in the civil war, typically burning Jews after capturing a village or small town. Had the Anglo-US support for the White Russians in the civil war been successful.

Churchill's intervention turned out to be a complete failure on all fronts. At first, Lloyd George and Wilson decided against approving a full-scale military action to overthrow the Bolsheviks. They were aware of the dangers such a path involved. Their minds had been greatly stimulated by the mutinies in the Entente forces. The growing working-class discontent at home and the worry that their own soldiers could be unwilling to fight had appeared to resolve the argument.

Since Lenin and Trotsky aimed to convert as many White soldiers as they could, it is evident that the phrase "every conceivable barbarity" did not apply to the civil war specifically. Instead, it was an allusion to the Bolshevik plan to have the Tsar and his family executed in July 1918, during the height of the civil war. The Politburo was worried that the White forces may capture the Tsar and his family and use them as battle emblems when it took this decision. Trotsky had first favored a trial, doubtless envisioning himself in the position of chief prosecutor exposing the historical transgressions of the Romanovs in front of a global audience. After all, it had been the English who had attempted to have their king executed first, also during a civil war. Following suit, the French executed both Louis XVI and Marie Antoinette in 1793. The Bolsheviks were adhering to accepted practice, but the demands of the civil war prevented a trial. The Black Hundreds' 'The Jews have killed our Tsar' civil war rallying cry made use of this to some extent.

He confided that the entire operation was a "useless, aimless, and ill-managed campaign" and that he "could not bear any longer to see splendid soldiers, who had given years of devoted sacrifice in France, uselessly killed." Earlier, a censor had read and revealed the contents of a letter Sherwood-Kelly had written to a friend in England. General Sir Henry Rawlinson presented him with the letter and informed him that it may have been grounds for a court martial, but that because of Sherwood-Kelly's stellar military record, he was willing to overlook the offense. However, he was to lose his position of leadership and be brought home to England.

It was terrible to read Sherwood-Kelly's open letter in the newspaper. He said that soldiers had been enlisted using fictitious information and plain lies. They had imagined it was a defensive, low-level relief operation meant to get troops trapped in the Arctic out of harm's way. Or to put it another way, a true humanitarian intervention. It didn't take long to realize that this was wrong. The soldiers were, in reality, "being used for offensive purposes on a large scale and far into the interior, in furtherance of some ambitious plan of campaign the nature of which we were not allowed to know," he claimed.

Churchill, who was obviously the 'High Official' in question, erupted in rage and demanded that Sherwood-Kelly be put on trial. A court martial was held as a result in Guildford, but a compassionate judge only gave him a harsh reprimand. Two weeks later, he gave his commission notice. He was given full military honors when he was buried in 1931 at the age of 51 after passing away from malaria.

At the national executive of the soviets on November 7, 1919—the second anniversary of the revolution—Trotsky declared that the civil war had been won, that the White generals had fled, and that while enlisted British prisoners of war had been freed, officers were being taken to Moscow. The Bolshevik leaders were encouraged by George Lansbury, a Labour MP and editor of the Daily Herald at the time, to release the soldiers but hold the officers hostage in order to get Britain to recognize the Soviet Union. Churchill was defeated. More bloodshed had resulted from his obsessions. Another offense noted in the book.

Little Kamenev is sneaky. Who dared to guess? Certainly not his wife or his close friends. Clare Sheridan was successful. Lenin and Trotsky must have found the Churchill connection amusing. Lenin sat for her, but he continued to work throughout. Although he called Churchill "our enemy who relies too much on the Court and the Army," she remembers him as "taciturn." She rebuffed Trotsky's invitation to ride along with him on his train to the front lines of the Civil War. In the late 1920s, she departed Moscow. She reportedly remarked, "I was given comfortable quarters in a requisitioned house," upon her return to England. Trotsky and Lenin are both good sitters. I spent 20 hours with Trotsky and 8 hours with Lenin. The latter caught her attention, and they started flirting. Trotsky asked her to tell her London friends that "when Trotsky kisses, he never bites," she later recounted.

I forgive you, child, as I would even if you had committed a crime, Sheridan's mother wrote to her upon her return. However, Churchill neglected to contact his cousin for a very long period, and she was briefly exiled to the United States. She, on the other hand, never forgot how Stalin "murdered all my friends." Churchill, on the other hand, did not appear overly moved by the murder of 90% of the Lenin Central Committee. When the next conflict broke out, this just made dealing with Stalin simpler.

Chapter 6:
Nine Days in May, 1926

Between the two world wars, there was a vast network of interconnected possibilities. The Russian Revolution occurred during a period of ideological and financial turmoil, which had an impact on Western politics. An increasing polarization between the socialist revolution and the fascist counter-revolution was observed in several European nations. The naïve belief of Woodrow Wilson that an Allied victory in the First globe War would'make the globe safe for democracy' quickly faded.

Churchill, on the other hand, never struggled to reconcile his conduct with intellect. He served as a metaphor for the agreement that had been reached between the industrial and mercantile bourgeoisie and the landed nobility since the latter's inception. He transitioned from one political party to the next and from one government position to the next with seemingly no effort.

Churchill was concerned when Labour was elected to office in November 1924 (even though it was a minority government). Based on forgeries intended to expose Ramsay MacDonald, the prime minister, as a secret Bolshevik, British Intelligence performed its duty and staged the overthrow of the government. Churchill reverted to being a Tory after noticing a slump in the Liberal party and made his way to the Treasury. His understanding of economics and finance? Nil. His first action was to disagree with his own civil officials over his first budget, who felt it was reckless. Sir Warren Fisher, the Treasury's permanent secretary, told Neville Chamberlain privately that Churchill "was a lunatic... an irresponsible child, not a grown man." Senior officials expressed their hopelessness by lamenting that they "never knew where they were or what hare W.C. will start."

Then, Churchill disagreed with Chamberlain—now in charge at the ministry of health—over social reforms that the latter believed were essential to enhancing the standard of living for workers. The poor law, local authority rates, health insurance, and the establishment of local health authorities were among the reforms proposed by Chamberlain. He had planned to introduce 23 measures over the course of three legislative sessions. Asserting that "the rich, whether idle or not, are already taxed in this country to the very highest point compatible with the accumulation of capital for further production," Churchill opposed the proposals.

One million miners were locked out nationwide on May Day 1926. Their cry for help to their coworkers could not be disregarded. The TUC General Council called for a general strike, though it carefully avoided using the exact words to avoid giving the wrong impression. Instead, it preferred the terms "coordinated industrial action" or "a national strike." A specially called conference backed the miners with a huge majority (99.87%). There were no undertones of revolt at all.

On May 6, 1926, Prime Minister Baldwin ramped up the rhetoric and said, "The General Strike is a challenge to Parliament and is the road to anarchy and ruin." The TUC's answer to the Conservative government's outright declaration of war was typical: "The General Council does not challenge the Constitution." The Council's only goal is to ensure that the miners have a fair quality of living. There is a labor dispute at the Council. It was undeniably true. However, despite the TUC's timidity, limitations in terms of structure and objectives, and lack of capability or desire for revolutionary action, the government's response was vehement.

However, at that point, the miners had grown bitter and angry over what they saw to be a betrayal by their coworkers, and they chose to submit rather than starve. However, they would never forget the people who had harmed them so severely. Churchill developed widespread animosity that was carried down from one generation to the next throughout Scotland, Wales, Northern England, considerable portions of London, and a few other major towns. Within weeks of the miners' defeat, the unions lost 500,000 members. The Labour administration, which was elected in 1929, refused to even consider nationalizing the mines. The prime minister, Ramsay MacDonald, claimed that the timing was not quite right. Due to their innate incapacity to comprehend, let alone combat, the capitalist crisis, the

Labour leaders simply defected to form a coalition government with the Tories and Liberals in the wake of the 1929 American and 1931 British financial crises, leaving only a small remnant of their party members in the House of Commons.

He was aware that some Liberal Party members were toying with the idea of turning the party into an anti-socialist center party. He warned against it, saying that "Liberalism, unless it is to be constructive, is a barren and impotent thing, and, reunion or no reunion, its destiny is the dust heap." He was adamantly opposed to this course of action. Despite the fact that many members of the parliamentary Labour Party, including its current leader, Keir Starmer, would want nothing more than a shift to the center, Scott's opinions continue to resonate in the pages of the newspaper he created a century after it was formed.

It should come as no surprise that Churchill became dependent on this drug. A terrible flaw, however, is that the majority of the British Labour movement has also been. Tony Benn and Jeremy Corbyn are two Labour MPs who have been willing to take on the archaic systems of monarchy, property, and power. All British political parties shared the belief that "they work well," so why make changes?

Chapter 7:
The Rise of Fascism

The numerous supporters of Adolf Hitler in the political establishments of Britain and the United States largely disregarded this essential aspect of his intellectual philosophy. Surprisingly, they exhibited passionate, subdued anti-Semitism. In France, where an anti-Semitic intellectual legacy that was deeply ingrained in most of the conservative and Catholic right predated Hitler, Hitler's political ideology was far more understood.

Fascism was viewed by Churchill as an extra-parliamentary movement with military groups of its own that might subdue the communists. He stayed steadfast on this until 1937. His admiration for Hitler and the strong, patriotic Hitler Youth was strong for a number of years, and he expressed ardent support for Mussolini and Franco. In addition to polishing and reusing parts of the defeated fascist states in Germany, Italy, and France, he supported using fascist remnants to defend Western colonial possessions in Asia and to maintain Greece's subjugation after the war. Police chiefs, military personnel, chiefs of intelligence, judges, and magistrates were kept on active duty to help win the Cold War.

The Socialist Party was a cohesive group. Socialists from both the revolutionary and moderate camps frequently disagreed about tactics, strategy, and the Russian Revolution, but they remained united. They received the most votes in the majority of important regions, including Emilia Romagna (60%) Piedmont (49.7%), Lombardy (45.9%), and Tuscany (41.7%). Southern Italy was won by the Liberal lists. The Parti Popular Italia (PPI), a christian-democratic party created in 1919 by a priest and supported by the Vatican to oppose the Socialists, received 20% of the vote and 100 seats in the Chamber of Deputies. It backed a number of social changes, including women's suffrage and proportional representation, but eventually split into rival pro- and anti-fascist sections. Pope Pius XI, who succeeded Peter in 1922, signed a concordat with Mussolini and later assisted fascist officials in Croatia in evading capture after World War II. Contrary to the Vatican's cooperation, several Catholic priests fought alongside the resistance and assisted certain Italian Jews in escaping their executioners.

Churchill visited Il Duce in 1927, five years after the fascists had taken control of Rome and Italy. Early on, he became convinced that Mussolini and Italian fascism were the only extra-parliamentary force that could overcome Bolshevism and its adherents in Europe. Fascists were able to mobilize the public in a way that traditional conservative parties were unable to. During his journey, he is reported to have said, "If I had been an Italian, I am sure I should have been wholeheartedly with you from the beginning to the end in your triumphant struggle against the bestial appetites and passions of Leninism." However, we have not yet had to deal with this threat in its most lethal form in England. We operate in a unique manner.

Unusually, Churchill chose to disregard Il Duce's colonial ambitions. Mussolini had made no secret of his aim to restore Italy's historical dominance over the Mediterranean, if not to equal that of Britain and France.

Due to this effusive praise, Churchill historians from both the liberal and conservative camps tend to avoid his more graphic pronouncements. Churchill's journey to Italy, according to Roy Jenkins, was part of a tourist excursion that included Vesuvius and culminated in "two encounters with Mussolini in Rome, after which he issued much too friendly statements." It would have been better for Churchill's reputation if he had stuck to this opinion, but as time went on he began to see [Mussolini] as a bulwark against Communism, which he feared would spread westward in post-war Europe, says Andrew Roberts. Churchill had criticized the Italian dictator for undermining the League of Nations in 1923. Because neither historian uses Churchill's own words, an examination of his actual love for Italian fascism is avoided.

Hitler's ascent to power had begun with an imitation of Mussolini. What became known as the Beer Hall Putsch of 1923 took place in Munich. The fascists' strategy was to kidnap the current Bavarian conservative state administration before setting up a rival National administration in Munich and enlisting the army to support them. Hitler had expected that the army would march with them as General Ludendorff had consented to do so. It was a grave error in judgment.

The ultra-nationalist philosophy of Mussolini pledged to restore Italy's greatness by building a contemporary Roman Empire. Fascist authority did not necessarily involve anti-Semitism, and numerous Jewish businesses were listed on the early membership lists of the Italian fascist party. Because of Hitler's own obsessions, German fascism made anti-Semitism a cornerstone of its policies.

During a time of defeats overseas, in Europe and China, political disputes and factional warfare inside the Bolshevik Party in the Soviet Union resulted in a win for Stalin's faction. The victorious Trotsky was banished from his country, stripped of his citizenship, and put into exile in Turkey. He was sent to the island of Prinkipo, where Byzantine emperors had jailed competitors, by Kemal Ataturk.

However, the balance of power did not originally favor fascism. The SPD received 6 million votes in the national elections of May 1924, the KPD about 4 million, the Centre Liberals 4 million, and the Nazis 2 million. Another election was called for December of that same year. The SPD currently has just under 8 million votes, down a million from the KPD, while the Center and Nazis both saw their support decrease to just 907,000. The pattern was largely the same in the May 1928 elections, with the Nazi vote falling to 810,000. There was a significant change when the Depression hit Germany hard. The fascist vote surged sevenfold to 6.5 million votes in September 1930, while the SPD received 8.5 million votes, the Communists 4.5 million votes, and the Centre 4 million votes.

His pleading was ignored. The left's failure left a lasting impression on members of both parties and the working class. With the backing of the vast majority of the German elite, Hitler was in power within two years. In the 1932 presidential elections, the KPD had supported Thaelmann. The SPD insisted on supporting von Hindenburg as the least of two evils despite refusing to even nominate its own candidate. After winning, he named Hitler the Reich Chancellor in January of the following year.

A sizable portion of the British Labour movement opposed colonial uprisings against the British empire. The group of Labourist intellectuals gathered at the Fabian Society gave MacDonald their full support. Bernard Shaw argued for the Empire in a number of writings. Declaring the existence of "higher and lesser civilizations" was his main contribution to Fabian thought on this topic. This was hardly a novel idea; Churchill, Leopold of Belgium, their French and German counterparts, Woodrow Wilson, and many others all had the same opinion.

Hitler used this notion of superior races domestically against Jews and later against Slavs in seized countries, giving it a new twist. They were subhuman, or untermenschen. The Nazi victory in 1933 signaled a sea change in global politics. The greatest state in Europe was now the center of revanchism against the imperialist nations that had humiliated it in 1919 and counter-revolution against the Bolsheviks. Goebbels, the first successful spin doctor of the 20th century, claimed that Germany had been expelled from the "comity of powerful political countries" as a result of the Versailles Treaty and that the main goal of the Nazis was "to unite the people and once more lead it back to the comity of nations." Mussolini uttered the same drivel during Hitler's triumphal visit to Rome in 1938, claiming that all the two nations desired was "justice, security, and peace for all."

Bolshevism's eradication, namely the eradication of Jewish Bolsheviks, was quickly proven to be Hitler and Mussolini's primary strategic objective in Europe. The military coup led by General Francisco Franco overthrew an elected Republican government in Spain, which was a coalition of left and progressive parties. This was the rehearsal for the bigger struggle that was being prepared. From the beginning, Churchill's stance was clear: "I will not pretend that, if I had to choose between Communism and Nazi-ism, I would choose Communism." He first embraced Franco, then Mussolini. Churchill's idiotic and reductionist remark did not accurately reflect the complexity of Spanish history. His antipathy toward the left rendered him unable to recognize how Franco's victory would only serve to tighten fascism's grip on Europe.

Churchill saw that this was not a rerun of the British General Strike of 1926, but rather a revolution supported by socialists, communists, and anarchists in Catalunya as well as socialists and communists who supported Moscow. Churchill supported the uniformed counterrevolution, along with the majority of European conservatives and the two fascist leaders. Stalin was concerned that there was no single party in complete control in Moscow to carry out Comintern commands. He was especially concerned about Catalunya, where the anarchists and the anti-Stalinist POUM (and their powerful backing in Soviet military intelligence) refused to toe the Moscow line. He permitted what amounted to a civil war on the left. Others, such as Jan Berzin and his network of internationalist agents headquartered in Western Europe and organized in the Fourth Department of the Red Army, were driven to success in Spain. They could see that it would be a victory over fascism and would even give the Soviet Union's demoralized working class new life.

Despite being uneasy and unsteady as always, the central authority in Madrid consented to provide the workers and residents who resisted the conspiracy with weaponry. The workers' parties were divided, despite the fact that all the elements for a revolutionary takeover were now in place. Under Franco's command, the military wasn't. the start of the civil war. We'll discover that Germany and Italy were crucial in providing Franco with the weapons, soldiers, and training he needed, perhaps most infamously with the Nazi destruction of the Basque town of Guernica. Non-intervention was advocated and practiced by Britain and France. The socialist leader of the Popular Front government in France, Léon Blum, was far too afraid to assist his compatriots in Spain. Numerous international brigades were organized to fight on the side of the Republicans.

Despite being unique, Spain's fate was similar to that of more than half of the twenty-eight European parliamentary or quasi-parliamentary democracies that had fallen prey to dictatorial governments by the start of 1939, as Julián Casanova points out. The Spanish revolution was met with separatist impulses in the Basque country and Catalunya, which intensified throughout periods of tyranny, which was a significant difference. Despite the support of Germany and Italy, the democratic goal of national self-determination at home and decolonization in Morocco would have helped to isolate and probably defeat Franco.

Churchill simply did not comprehend a lot during this time. He failed to recognize the steel curtain adorned with swastikas that threatened Europe and that Hitler's rise signified a renewal and consolidation of German empire because he was enamored with Mussolini, fascinated by Hitler's organization, and a supporter of Franco's victory in Spain. By the time he realized the seriousness of the situation, it was too late to take any action.

Churchill wrote another article for the Evening Standard on 2 October 1936, which was two months later. This time, he focused on the Republican side's murder of hostages in Madrid. Civil wars are rarely attractive. It depends on your stance. El Socialista issued a powerful editorial the day following Churchill's essay headlined "Moral Obligations in War" that expressed the Republican camp's vehement opposition to the Madrid executions: "The life of an enemy who surrenders is unassailable; no combatant can dispose of that life." But the rebels don't act that way. No big deal. This is the way we ought to act. Churchill acknowledged that the gangs of Franco "shoot a percentage of their prisoners taken in arms" on a regular basis, but he claimed that this was not equal to what he called the "tortures and fiendish outrages in the lowest pit of human degradation" carried out by Republicans. The British public opinion rating both sides equally would be an error in truth and judgment, he said in his conclusion. To put it another way, Franco was superior to the Republicans. Churchill, who was prejudiced by class and imperialism, supported European fascism wholeheartedly in its fight against the left.

Chapter 8:
Japan's Bid for Mastery in Asia

A future conflict with the United States and Britain was all but assured after Japan declared war on China in July 1937, sparking the Second World War. Japanese troops had taken control of several of the most significant ports and cities, including Shanghai and Nanjing, by December of the same year. One million people in China were currently under occupation.

The Japanese threat was never taken seriously by Churchill. He stated there was not even the "tiniest chance" of conflict with Japan in his lifetime in the late 1920s. He didn't realize Japan was a threat until it was too late. Before that, Britain had seen the Japanese as a potential ally in discussions about the shifting balance of power in Asia. The two island monarchs were steadfast friends from 1902 through 1922. Japan participated in the First World War as an Entente country. The Foreign Office was anxious when the time came to renew Britain's treaty with Japan. Churchill said that refusing to renew it might very well be viewed as unfriendly behavior.

Japan continued to be an underappreciated worldwide participant in the interwar period. Japanese politicians fell into a similar trap when they were treated by Western colonial powers with a combination of condescension, racism, and plain disrespect. They believed they could do it. They considered the naval war they won in 1905 against Tsarist Russia to be the greatest of its kind in modern times. It is unusual for a large Western imperial state to completely annihilate its whole fleet at sea in the course of a single afternoon. Marshal Admiral Tg Heihachir, a skilled strategist who had spent seven years training as a naval cadet in Britain (1871–78), was responsible for this victory. He idolized Nelson, therefore it delighted him when the English press afterwards referred to him as "the Nelson of the East."

While British colonies like Australia and Canada had more than 3 million square miles to feed 6.5 million mouths each, other Japanese militarists questioned why their nation should be content with

142,270 square miles to feed 60 million people. Japan's determination to invade China and destroy British assets in Asia in order to push back their main Pacific adversary, the United States, was motivated by a lethal imperialist logic. The precise sequence for the final section of their plan was still up in the air. Because of this, the Second World War started on July 7, 1937, when Japan invaded China, and it ended on August 6, 1945, when an atomic bomb was launched on Hiroshima in Japan. It originated in Asia and extended to Europe before making its way back to Asia with Japan's rash, if not entirely irrational, attack on Pearl Harbor on December 7, 1941.

It wasn't just a case of an island kingdom going up against a failing continental power on its own when they invaded China. While their Axis allies, particularly Germany, seized Europe and erected the swastika on the Kremlin, the imperial officials in Tokyo believed they could take China. Even a triumph summit in Vladivostok had been arranged by Hitler and Hirohito.

This significant fight, like so many others (the assassination in Sarajevo that started the European Civil War in 1914 comes to mind), began as an unanticipated conflict between Japanese and Chinese soldiers on the Marco Polo Bridge in July 1937, about 30 kilometers south of Beijing. Tokyo instructed local officers on the scene to settle the issue quickly, but the gunfire and some casualties continued for three days. An armistice was negotiated by officers on the ground from both sides, resulting in a three-week break.

Senior and less fervent General Staff members counseled caution. Another battle, this one on Kanchazu Island in the Amur River between Japanese forces and Soviet Red Army soldiers, had the generals Ishiwara and Torashiro worried. The Soviet Union had lost two gunboats. The generals resisted sending more soldiers to Northern China and warned of a potential Soviet counteroffensive. The emperor briefly supported this position after expressing his displeasure with individuals in his entourage who supported the expansionists.

However, following additional negotiations, Prime Minister Konoe and his Cabinet made a U-turn and decided to send more troops to

Northern China. The journalist and academic Ozaki Hotsumi, who had been chosen to serve for Soviet military intelligence by Richard Sorge, is one of Konoe's most important advisors on China. Sorge is now well-established in Tokyo. Both of these men indirectly contributed to the decision to send soldiers to China, which lessened the military pressure on the Soviet Union.

The 1911 revolution in China resulted in the overthrow of the rotting, ripe-rotten Qing Dynasty, the proclamation of a republic, and the ascent of Dr. Sun Yat-sen, a well-known nationalist democrat who had long campaigned against the Qing on both a literary and a military level. He called the Manchu invasion of China in the seventeenth century a terrible national tragedy and, in an effort to break with his own nation's gloomy past, he himself became a Christian. During Sun Yat-sen's years of exile in Japan, the politics of the country had become more radical, which contributed to the collapse of the Chinese state and the Qing dynasty, which had ruled for more than three centuries.

When Sun Yat-sen passed away from cancer in March 1925, it was a watershed moment that Moscow failed to recognize. Growing hostilities between the CCP and the GMD's right wing, which was commanded by Sun Yat-sen's brother-in-law Chiang Kai-shek, were disregarded. Sun Yat-sen's widow, Soong Ching-ling, was a member of the GMD's left-wing faction, but it was not as strong. The Chinese communists, who were heavily influenced by Moscow, followed a suicidal Comintern directive to maintain their allegiance to the GMD despite all the challenges. The terrible expenses of carrying out this directive led to Mao Zedong's hegemonic control over the party and a change in tactic.

Most Chinese leaders realized that the United Front was no longer viable by this point. April 1927 saw brutal GMD suppression of CCP organizations in Shanghai, and Guangzhou three years later. A Comintern observer watched as the peasant organization was disarmed and destroyed by landlords with support from the GMD but did nothing. In addition to witnessing the calamity, Mao Zedong, who had been ordered by his party to work full-time at the Peasant Movement Training Institute since 1924, was also enraged by the

Comintern's inaction. In contravention of Stalin's orders, he left the Institute and went on to engage with the Hunan peasant movement. His essay, "An Investigation of the Peasant Movement in Hunan," quickly rose to prominence in the Chinese revolutionary movement for its analysis of the class differences among peasants and refusal to view the vast majority of rural people (who make up the vast majority of the population of the nation) as an undifferentiated mass.

The Shanghai massacre and the simultaneous murders of at least 10,000 communists in numerous other cities served as the catalyst for the start of a 10-year civil war in China. The GMD was on the rise and was now being paid for by both urban and rural investors. After the incident on April 12, spirited discussions inside the CCP gradually resulted in a shift in perspective. The communists had lost the cities, and the Blueshirts, a powerful fascist organization in the GMD that specialized in targeted executions and atrocities, had taken control. A choice was necessitated by the GMD's annihilation of the Changsha Soviet in 1934–195.

Barely a month after capturing Shanghai, Japanese tanks stormed Nanjing early on December 13th, and General Matsui's forces occupied the city. There was no opposition. The GMD government had made the decision to go back. The wealthy and prosperous had followed in their footsteps. Poor people were abandoned to their destiny. The six weeks that followed were sheer horror. Without a doubt, this was one of the worst crimes committed during the Second World War, but neither Churchill's 1,065-page memoirs of the conflict, published in 1959, nor the 947-page classic account of the conflict by French historian Henri Michel, La Seconde Guerre Mondiale, published in 1975, make even a passing mention of it. There is a slight improvement among American war historians. A single mention in one instance, a paragraph in another.

The press and intellectual life were both subject to a forceful conformism as well. These divine punishments were aimed at communists, labor and peasant campaigners. Tosuiken, or the autonomy of supreme command, was a prerogative of Hirohito that was never ceded. He was jubilant and triumphalist about the success of the Kwantung Army, but he was a little worried about how the

West would react to the invasion of Manchuria. His unwillingness to condemn the violent crimes committed by his young officers in China inspired them to commit even worse excesses in the name of "divine Japan." Following the rapes and killings in Nanjing, troops and officers offered a collective toast to the emperor as General Matsui rode his horse through empty Nanjing streets while being followed by his men. To be safe, a cautious Prince Asaka had commanded that everyone who lived near the triumph march be killed.

Hirohito participated in daily decision-making as the conflict escalated into a full-scale war, approving the deployment of poison gas and "signing off" on operations against guerrilla bases that came to be known as the sanko, or the "three alls": kill all, burn all, plunder all. Hirohito was a "real war leader," according to Bix, who "carefully examined and sanctioned the policies, strategies, and orders for waging wars of aggression."

The GMD's failure to protect Shanghai or Nanjing, choosing to escape rather than fight, left a lasting impression on Chinese national memory. Was there any hope for redemption if the 'nationalist' party and government had failed so miserably? In response to the Japanese invasion in 1937, the GMD and the CCP once more agreed to form a United Front and put their differences aside until the Japanese were driven out of the country.

The emperor was about to make a crucial choice in Tokyo in 1941 that would influence the future of both his own nation and China. The Japanese political and military elites had sharply divergent views on whether it was appropriate to start a war with the United States. A time restriction for diplomacy was being pushed by the military. Even those who did not wish to prolong the war were annoyed by the US sanctions against Japan, but Prime Minister Konoe, who was legally Hirohito's only advisor, opposed any further hostilities. But the militarists were obstinate.

Sugiyama and the high command had come to an agreement on a strategy that depended on seizing South and East Asian colonies of the British, French, and Dutch for both strategic and economic reasons. At the same time, "we shall cooperate with Germany and Italy to destroy the unity of the United States and Britain." Since it "would see us link up Europe and Asia, guiding the situation to our advantage," this would put Japan in an impregnable position. If we are successful here, there may be a chance that the conflict will end, at least with the United States.

The Soviet Union might invade from the north, Hirohito said on the third day of the summit, and he stressed that a three-front war would be very difficult to maintain. Regarding this concern, his generals reassured him. Winter was rapidly approaching, and the Red Army was not insane enough to send its divisions out into the snow without any other concerns.

The emperor interfered on every level, even overseeing and scrutinizing the specifics of the war rescript that would be delivered when they began the invasion. At further sessions in November, the emperor was completely convinced of the need to battle the United States. The document was created by a Chinese classics expert employed by the court. It was quite evident that the Kingdom of Japan was preparing to destroy Anglo-American imperialism in Asia "for its existence and self-defense."

The British Empire suffered its worst defeat in the Asian War with the loss of Singapore in February 1942 to a Japanese army half the size of Britain's "impregnable fortress." Hitler's communication to the Japanese foreign minister, Yousuke Matsuoka, was deciphered by British codebreakers a year earlier. The head of the German army insisted on having the Japanese attack Singapore and seize Malaya. He was certain that Britain would suffer a fatal blow from which it would never fully recover. Churchill arrogantly thought it impossible to capture Singapore. The British naval base was well-equipped and robust. The hinterland's woodlands were impassable. How were the 'little Japs' supposed to cross them? He said Singapore was the "Gibraltar of the Far East," which is a bit of a ridiculous comparison considering that only Franco's neutrality toward the British and Americans prevented the fall of Gibraltar. In the end, the Japanese took control of the naval dockyards. Churchill had no right to assume that a naval base with few warships—the majority of them were in the Middle East—could protect itself. The "little Japanese" quickly advanced into the trees as well. The British Army was captured along with 90,000 men on February 15, 1942. Churchill placed the blame on the local leaders, yet he was the one who underestimated Japan. Regardless of what happened to Japan in the end, this setback signaled the beginning of the end for the British Empire.

Chapter 9:
The War in Europe: From Munich to Stalingrad

He must have been discouraged by the fact that Churchill himself had not rejected the possibility of making a deal with Hitler a few months earlier. He made a point of endorsing the Chamberlain government's foreign policy at the Conservative Party Conference in Scarborough in October 1937. Churchill counseled, "Let us indeed support the foreign policy of our Government, which commands the trust, comprehension and the comradeship of peace-loving and law-respecting nations in all parts of the world." There had been disagreements on rearmament in the past, but these had been amicably resolved. He told his readers in the Evening Standard the following week that "War is NOT imminent."

British pacifism, exemplified by the Peace Pledge Union and an opposition to rearmament, much alone a new war, has its roots in the horror of that conflict. Politicians from both the Tories and the Labour Party knew this. Many people did not perceive Chamberlain's accommodation of the fascist leader as such until the Anschluss and the takeover of Czechoslovakia started to focus minds. Only until the summer of 1939 did public support for the prime minister's attempt to negotiate with Hitler start to erode. Because of his repeated calls for "peace," Hitler was seen as someone who was attempting to prevent a new conflict, which continued to mislead others. Even after his resignation in 1940 and Churchill's appointment as his replacement, Chamberlain continued to have enormous support within the Conservative Party.

Divisions in the British Parliament persisted after the 1938 Munich Agreement between Germany and Britain, which agreed to further concessions to Hitler (including Czechoslovakia). Churchill and the appeasers differed on what Nicolson had already mentioned. Dealing with the German upstart would best serve the class interests of those who dominated Britain and of those on whose behalf they did so, according to Chamberlain, Halifax, and the businesses who supported them. Churchill realized that Britain needed to keep up with the Germans on the rearmament front before the others did, if not in order to prepare for war, then at the very least to sustain pressure in negotiations.

He had come to understand by 1939 that the British Empire and British sovereignty were actually at risk. He intended to present a carrot with a distinct stick in view because of this. The British were not opposed to this if it was a part of a bigger settlement because the Germans had made it known that they wanted their former colonies back. In order to advance the interests of both the fascist dictatorships and the capitalist democracies, namely France and Britain, both sides intended that the Soviet Union be vanquished first.

Stalin and his henchmen made the decision to cleanse the senior ranks of the Red Army six months later, in June 1937. Generals Uborevich, Yakir, Primakov, Putna, and Edleman were also executed on 'treason' charges together with Tukhachevsky. The following year, Marshal Yegorov, who had argued with Tukhachevsky in the war simulations, vanished and was subsequently declared dead. In November 1938, Marshal Blyukher, the head of the Soviet forces in the Far East, was put to death. At the Frunze Military Academy, General Vatzetis, a prominent commanding commander during the Civil War, was detained between his lecture and the questions.

For a long time, Churchill had maintained that fascism was, on the whole, acceptable as long as it used its power and popular support to fight against Bolshevism on all fronts, both domestically and abroad. As was mentioned in the chapter before, he had backed Franco and, consequently, the Italian and German involvement in the Spanish Civil War to assure victory. Ever had any doubts in his mind? Did he truly believe it could end in Spain? Did no one warn him that the Italians and Germans were using Spain as a staging ground for a larger conflict? If so, there is no indication of it in his writings from the time, which simply express a religious wish for Spain to unite under Franco and the Catholic Church as the war's winners. Although it chose not to intervene, the French Popular Front government provided the Republic with moral support.

Wehrmacht officers insisted that Norway must be conquered first, which caused Hitler enormous annoyance and delayed the attack of France. Due to its 15,000 miles of coastline, it was weak. A blockade had already been imposed by the British Navy, preventing access to the Scandinavian peninsula from the North Sea. This put at risk the flow of Swedish iron and ore supplies, which were crucial to the rearmament program and ammunition manufacturers in Germany.

Over the course of a weekend, Denmark was busy thanks to two calls from Berlin. The socialist government of Sweden quickly declared its neutrality. The Norwegians put up a valiant fight but were defeated. The king, his family, and courtiers were flown to London by a British submarine.

The progression of events was simple. The Dutch and Belgian embassies in Berlin were called to the foreign ministry on May 10, 1940, where Ribbentrop advised them that their nations would soon be occupied and that they should wish their sovereignties goodnight. The Dutch dithering. The Luftwaffe struck Rotterdam four days later, killing 800 civilians. The Dutch gave up the next morning. Their monarch ran away to London. Following the capture of Belgium by the enemy a fortnight later, France fell. In the same railway cabin where the Germans had surrendered in 1918, Hitler and his generals received the French capitulation. For the benefit of the German press, the Führer pranced and hopped around. Now was the time to exact revenge for the humiliating Treaty of Versailles. More than any other single incident during the war, the quick triumph in France improved Hitler's reputation. He was "in utter bliss after his grandiose triumphs," Goebbels declared. The generals would rarely disagree with his military choices during the following few years. However, the political and military authorities of the Third Reich would later regret not eliminating the British when the chance presented itself.

How to dispatch British forces as quickly as possible out of France and back home was the key concern for Churchill and his generals once it fell. Germans were helpful in this case. General Heinz Guderian, a notable expert on tank warfare and a supporter of the blitzkrieg, had been advancing relentlessly until he was told by Hitler to stop, much to his chagrin. The Führer's tragic choice allowed Britain to use whatsoever means necessary to rescue as many men as possible.

Hitler alone made the choice. It's hard to think that decision was only based on military considerations. By interfering with already-running operations, the Führer had already irritated his military officers. He gave the command for the German troops to cease when they were thirteen kilometers from Dunkirk. General Halder, the head of the German armed forces, wrote in his journal about his frustration: "The tanks and military formations are standing motionless, as if nailed to the place between Bethune and Saint-Omer, under command from the highest level, and are not allowed to strike... It will take weeks to empty this pocket as things are. It seriously harms both our reputation and our future goals. Whatever his motivations, Hitler made a political choice.

Stalin believed that the Non-Aggression Pact might continue, in contrast to the Germans who considered it as necessary but short-lived. Lev Bezymensky, a Soviet historian and combat veteran, spoke with Marshal Zhukov in 1966. Owen Matthews quotes from this interview. Zhukov and others had forewarned Stalin of worrying German military deployments in January 1941. Stalin kindly enquired Hitler in a letter about the veracity of these rumors. They were, Hitler said, but he swore, "On my honor as a head of state, my troops are deployed... for other purposes." The areas of Western and Central Germany are heavily bombed by the English, who can readily monitor them from the air. I therefore felt it necessary to deploy sizable force contingents to the east so they could covertly rearm and reorganize. Stalin had faith in him.

The German Army resolutely marched to its cemetery on June 22, 1941. Two of the world's most formidable armies would engage in battle from the Baltic to the Black Sea for the ensuing four years. The Panzer divisions quickly took control of an area the size of Germany. Optimism was high. Summer still lingered. Many generals and senior officers who had been detained but not killed between 1937 and 1938 had been freed by Stalin. From the prison, they immediately went to the front.

The Habsburgs, Ottomans, Romanovs, and Hohenzollerns were among the four royal dynasties that fell as a result of the First World War, along with three other sizable empires. The British and French had taken over the Middle Eastern remnants of their empires, Woodrow Wilson had established new nation-states in Europe, and the Russian Revolution had spread to many of the adjacent Tsarist colonies, which were either voluntarily or unwillingly incorporated into the Soviet Union.

All of this was in danger in 1942 as Field Marshal Rommel's German Army advanced into British colonies. As always, when imperial territories were in danger, Churchill was very alarmed. Though he was aware of the prospect, he did not fully understand that even an Allied triumph would not be enough to save the blood-spattered Empire. Beyond the strains brought on by the continuous wars in Europe and the East, the company was now morally, politically, and financially bankrupt. Arab nationalists, particularly those in Baghdad, Cairo, Alexandria, and Damascus, were open about their desire for a German victory.

Japan had already conquered Indochina in 1940 with the assistance of Vichy France. The colony was still run by the latter, sparing the Japanese a lot of trouble. This period of dual imperialism in Indochina from 1940 to 1945 served as the best possible example of the similarities between Axis fascism and European imperialism. Additionally, it was the sole instance of violent resistance to Japan (or more specifically, to dual imperialism) by communists and certain nationalist forces outside of China. In other places, organized nationalists favored taking the Japanese at their word or, at the least, to utilize them as a weapon against long-standing European empires. Ahmed Sukarno used the Japanese to fight the Dutch in Java, and Subhas Chandra Bose and, through Gandhi, the British, in India.

The careless General Claude Auchinleck wrote a personal letter to Churchill in which he apologized piteously, if somewhat incoherently, and accepted full responsibility (as was proper) for the mishap. He was officially deposed and dispatched to the east. The Auk's bruised ego would be soothed and healed by sycophantic Indian officers. But in actuality, the issue was considerably more complex than a single person's errors.

With support from the Cabinet, Churchill, Attlee, and Bevin—the so-called worker's leader in the Cabinet—decided to keep the report a secret. They disclosed that it was a "secret" paper to Parliament. This was an egregious falsehood. The publishing may encourage "anti-

Americanism" in the nation if it were perceived as an unwelcome American meddling, according to the justification offered to the Cabinet. This justification is hardly plausible. The governing classes and certain parts of the Foreign Office were the major targets of the anti-Americanism that prevailed at the time. The report's suppression can only have been motivated by a worry that it may spark a strike or, at the very least, raise class consciousness. In a hurry, the government established its own Committee on the Coal Mining Industry. Even when its conclusions were moderately worded, they would not be significantly different.

On the banks of the Volga, outside of Stalingrad (now Volgograd), the most crucial combat of the entire European war was about to start. Hitler had commanded the Fourth Panzer division and the Sixth Army to take the city at any costs. They had troops from Romania and Hungary manning the rear as additional backup.

The battle at Stalingrad lasted for more than five months, and the tactics that had to be used were those that Trotsky and Tukhachevsky had almost mastered in the civil war two decades before, as detailed by John Erickson in his three essential volumes on the Red Army. Not only has Stalingrad been memorialized in several books and films, but so have other significant battles from the conflict. Their quality varies. There is only one literary classic: Vasily Grossman's Life and Fate.

On August 23, 1942, the Battle of Stalingrad got underway during the summer. On 2 February 1943, in the dead of winter, it came to an end. It was the bloodiest combat of the Second World War with an estimated 2 million casualties. The capitulation incensed Hitler. The Soviet Union now had a field marshal, twenty-two generals, and a quarter of a million soldiers, mostly German but also including Italians, Spaniards, Hungarians, and Romanians. The liberation of Stalingrad and Moscow. Then came Leningrad.

The German high command committed to Operation Citadel, a struggle to defeat the Red Army on the Soviet salient around Kursk in western Russia, in an effort to exact revenge for the loss at Stalingrad. This time, Soviet forces were well-organized and had a high level of morale. Before the Red Army defenses were seriously breached, the German onslaught was stopped. Hitler ended the conflict after three days because of the significant German losses. The war's largest tank combat took place there. The Red Army had won the battle. Dmitri Shostakovich, whose Leningrad Symphony and astounding string quartets were an ode to people who had persisted under the worst of circumstances, was comparable to Grossman in a different media.

Chapter 10:
The Indian Cauldron

India saw ongoing unrest during the interwar era. The majority of Indians thought the 1919 reforms were poorly intended and offered very little, despite the fact that they had promised expanded political participation of Indians in government while denying them authority. The secretary of state for India at the time, Edwin Montagu, had stated in Parliament that "the gradual development of self-governing institutions, with a view to the progressive realization of responsible government in India as an integral part of the British Empire," was to take place. Pressure from below increased as a result.

While out of office, Churchill bitterly opposed the new law. The Act established a limited level of provincial autonomy, with each province's governor having the reserve authority to dissolve "irresponsible" administrations. With the important exceptions of Punjab and Bengal, where secular-conservative, landlord-run parties won majorities, the limited franchise was slightly expanded, and the ruling Congress Party practically won every province in the 1937 elections.

Following these elections, Britain entered a war two years later. The Congress leaders demanded that all provincial governments resign in protest because they were not consulted before India was drawn into the conflict and they refused to support the war. All of this supported Churchill's preconceptions. He merely resisted understanding Indian realities.

From the end of the First World War until the late 1930s, the number of demonstrations and acts of resistance increased yearly. Gandhi himself was a fervent supporter of the Empire throughout his time in South Africa. Since he shared Churchill's belief that "the British Empire existed for the benefit of the world," the Indian lawyer was not at all ashamed of his role as a recruitment sergeant during the First globe War. When he went back to India and recreated himself as a political deity, he changed his mind. On a moral level,' he was pleased to mobilize the masses. He would leave politics, particularly

Nehru and Patel, to handle matters of state. However, he always gave his approval when they needed it under pressing situations (such as the partition of India and the Indian annexation of Kashmir).

Another avoidable mistake was made by London when it decided to enter the Second World War without consulting any of the country's elected officials. The British miscalculated the shift in the populace's and some of their leaders' attitudes. Things may have turned out differently if they had contacted Gandhi and Nehru and offered them a fig leaf to support the war. After several months of lengthy internal deliberations (which exposed a powerful anti-war section headed by the Bengali leader, Subhas Chandra Bose), the Congress leaders decided to resign from office because they believed they had been treated poorly.

Gandhi wailed and dragged his feet, but the Bengali Congress leader Subhas Chandra Bose, who had always been vehemently opposed to the idea of lending any support to the British war, went on the attack. He was the most extreme nationalist in the entire senior command of the Congress. He started to develop a strategy that was more inspired by the leaders of the Chittagong Armory Raid than by Gandhi. Bose did not think that peaceful means could be successful. While they were fine at moments, the situation was grave at the moment. India had been insulted by Britain when it once more took its young men away to engage in inter-imperialist conflicts. Bose started looking into all options in order to build an Indian National Army.

1942 saw Churchill approve the dispatch of left-leaning British ambassador to Moscow Sir Stafford Cripps to India to meet with leaders like Nehru, Gandhi, and others to beg them to aid Britain. He could make a verbal commitment of independence following the conflict if they were willing. Before Cripps could leave, though, devastating news from South-East Asia arrived: Singapore had been overthrown. Churchill cited the field soldiers as the culprits. Because there were so many men in Singapore, the British Army felt that they should have done better in their defense. It was a huge blow, as was emphasized above.

Churchill placed his faith in Jinnah and Sikandar Hyat Khan, the leader of the Unionist Party and elected premier of the Punjab, a region vital to the war effort in terms of manpower and because it is the granary of India, after Cripps returned empty-handed, as the main candidates for a stable Indian army. As soon as Cripps returned, Churchill declared, "I despise Indians. He was voicing a long-held belief, but in this case he was speaking of the Hindus who had severely disappointed him: "They are a beastly people with a beastly religion."

Bose and Hitler only met once, and it didn't go well. After reading Mein Kampf, he concluded that Churchill's derogatory statements on Indians were not all that different from those made by the Führer. He disagreed with Hitler, but he was instructed that he should head to Tokyo as quickly as possible since the Japanese might be a better option. Bose followed the suggestions. Japanese people were much more receptive. Bose had his INA when Singapore fell. In Burma, a cohesive, secular force engaged in combat with British army formations.

Even though jute sales were not as profitable as opium's trade did not require gunboats, the Crimean War and the US Civil War both witnessed significant increases in demand and earnings. Four decades after the East India Company's initial shipment from Bengal in 1795, pure jute yarn was produced and marketed in Dundee. The Parsi magnate Sir Dorabji Jamsetji Tata was one of the four Indian members of the Indian Industrial Commission (1916–18), which by 1918 had ten members, only four of whom were Indian. The report noted that "the annual average value of the jute trade to Bengal has been computed at 10,000,000 pounds" and added that "the association of the Calcutta jute industry with the east coast of Scotland has throughout remained intimate."

One of the most serious accusations made against Churchill in regards to India is that he was to blame for the Bengal famine. On this topic, Indian historians disagree. Some people believe that Churchill's verbal assaults on Gandhi and his absolute hatred for him are even bigger sins. However, being impolite rarely has any effect. It is accurate to say that Churchill attacked the Indian leader, branding him a "malignant subversive fanatic" and "a seditious Middle Temple lawyer, now posing as a fakir of a type well known in the East, striding half-naked up the steps of the Viceregal palace." Gandhi was deemed "dangerous" by the governor of Bombay, Lord Willingdon, since he was a "Bolshevik."

However, if Gandhi had been a fanatical subversive Bolshevik, the British would have had far more trouble in the 1920s. When Churchill said that Gandhi's 1932 "fast unto death" was a hoax and claimed that glucose was being dissolved in the water he drank, some people became quite upset. Churchill and Linlithgow conversation on this topic today reads like satire.

There is no questioning Churchill's callousness: phrases like "Indians breed like rabbits"—commonly used in reference to Irish Catholics—were criminally negligent. When it became evident what was happening in Bengal, the failure to proclaim a state of emergency there, quickly change the policies that were depriving the populace of food, and import rice and flour from other parts of the nation was equally criminal. Churchill was undoubtedly accountable for this atrocity, but so was the entire wartime alliance, including Attlee and Bevin. They never voiced disapproval or offered solutions to the issue. Churchill believed that the numbers were being inflated by dishonest Indians, but in reality, the British were frantically attempting to prevent the information from spreading throughout India or reaching Britain.

In his account of the war, Churchill did not make any explicit mention of this atrocity. His vague and inaccurate comment that "No great portion of the world population was so effectively protected from the horrors and pitfalls of the world war as were the peoples of Hindustan" may have been the result of subconscious guilt. They were supported by our tiny island throughout the struggle.

Despite all the catastrophes, the 1943 harvest was only 5% below average compared to years prior. Millions did not perish from a shortage of food. Simply put, the food was rendered inaccessible on orders from Delhi's top imperial officials, who were carrying out London's directives. Priority was given to those working on daily military production and feeding the army. The Bengali government's recommendation that citizens stock up on grain following the Japanese advance, which further reduced supplies, was another contributing reason. Additionally, there were Chinese and US forces in Assam and northeast Bengal, which added to the food shortage.

Where the food should be sent was clear to Churchill. His close buddy and scientist friend Fred Lindemann (aka "The Prof"), who is of German descent, was his principal advisor on food distribution in Britain. He wasn't well liked by everyone. Many in Whitehall were enraged by his haughtiness and proximity to Churchill because they believed that 'the Prof' was misusing, twisting, and unnecessarily condensing their properly researched facts and figures in order to appease Churchill's preconceptions and instincts.

Viceroy Linlithgow was replaced in October 1943 by Wavell, whose imperial career includes the suppression of the Arab Revolt in Palestine and catastrophic defeat in Malaya, Singapore, and Burma. Viceroy Linlithgow's stance toward the widespread hunger had been to ignore it as far as possible. He has previously served in Somaliland, Cyprus, and Kenya. Many of the officers in the imperial legions traveled along this route. Churchill moved him to New Delhi to get rid of him because he thought Wavell was a letdown of a military leader (i.e., Wavell disagreed with Churchill). As "a good average colonel" who would have made "a good chairman of a Tory association," Churchill thought of him. This seemed somewhat unjust.

The British government offered 150,000 tons of rice in exchange for 400,000 tons of wheat in March 1944. Wavell was able to remove 200,000 tons from the war cabinet in June, but he felt that this was still insufficient. Midway through 1944, Churchill personally requested US assistance, but cargo had already been diverted to the European conflict.

Churchill noted that the starvation of the "anyhow under-fed Bengalis" was less serious than that of the "sturdy Greeks," but the war council was unfazed. Winston "hates India and everything to do with it so much that he can see nothing but waste of shipping space," Amery wrote in his journal.

By the end of the year, it looked that Wavell's intervention had stabilized the situation in Calcutta, but widespread famine persisted in the countryside. Chronic fabric shortages made the plight of the rural poor worse as winter drew closer, resulting in numerous deaths that were not only homeless and famished but also almost naked. However, the starvation was purportedly under control for propaganda purposes. Despite Wavell's appeals, the war cabinet continued to oppose food shipments. As infections spread across a population that was already vulnerable, death rates rose in the first half of 1944; malaria deaths peaked in November. During 1944, 2 million additional people perished from hunger, illness, and exposure.

To prevent the creation of a separate Muslim state called Pakistan, the Cabinet Mission to India of the Attlee administration published their plan for a united, independent India with extensive regional autonomy on May 16, 1946. The suggestion was first accepted by the Congress leadership, but they soon started to change their minds on the grounds that the Muslim League would have too much representation. Nehru categorically opposed the plan on July 10. Four weeks later, the Muslim League organized a "direct-action day" to push for the establishment of Pakistan.

Many years prior, the Bengali social reformer Ram Mohan Roy had remarked, "What Bengal thinks today, India thinks tomorrow." He was referring to the Bengali people's vibrant culture and robust political consciousness. The division of the subcontinent was predicted by the riots of 1946. They occurred as a community that had been brutalized by years of privation finally started to fall apart, during a time of renewed scarcity. The Muslim League hartal was the reason, but the city's "very specific and identifiable tensions" were the real reason. The control of city blocks, alleyways, and neighborhoods was the subject of a "localized battle."

Churchill studied Macaulay's essays during his first visit to India in 1898 and was greatly impressed by them—until he discovered the historian's prohibitions on the patriarch of the Churchill dynasty. Then Macaulay turned "rogue." The second Governor-General chosen by the East India Company, Warren Hastings, was the target of Macaulay's article. Churchill did not record his opinions on the subject. Churchill, who was based in India, must have read it. Did he highlight the last sentence so he could remember it later? Most likely not. He ought to have. "Those who look on his character without favor or malice will pronounce that, in the two great elements of all social virtue, respect for the rights of others, and sympathy for the sufferings of others, he was deficient," Macaulay wrote in the conclusion of his article. His morals were a little slack.

Edmund Burke's vicious impeachment speech in the House of Lords in 1788, which accused Hastings of committing "high crimes and misdemeanors" on behalf of the House of Commons, served as the impetus for Macaulay's article. There is no question that Hastings was a wild man. In those early years of British control in Bengal and the surrounding areas, he robbed at will because he wanted to gain money. He upset polite society by robbing the wealthy in order to enrich himself.

Even then, the idea of using the House of Lords as "a sacred temple" to fight tyranny was absurd, and Burke's blatant flattery was ineffective. Hastings received acquittal. He was now insolvent as a result of the nearly two-year-long process. Reputational damage was never entirely repaired. Churchill and his collaborator in colonial war crimes, Attlee, were never mentioned as candidates for impeachment.

Chapter 11:
Resistance and Repression

Effective and persistent anti-fascist resistance in Germany itself was mostly confined to the clandestine Communist Party of Germany (KPD). Of course, there were a few really brave and tenacious students who publicly criticized the administration and gave their lives in the process. Despite KPD efforts, armed conflict as well as any real public defiance as opposed to symbolic opposition were impossible. Millions of KPD supporters, voters, and members had registered, the majority of them being manufacturing workers. Hitler took power as chancellor in January 1933, and soon after that, the KPD was outlawed, its offices were sealed, its leaders were sought out, and its members were subjected to torture, arrest, and even death.

Hitler would not rule for very long, according to KPD officials, and for a while, communists and fascists clashed in the streets. This came to an abrupt end. The KPD reorganized and resisted as best they could as they realized the extent of the setback and its repercussions. Being the eyes and ears of both Moscow and London was one way the resistance in fascist Germany manifested itself. The KPD sympathizers who had infiltrated the top echelons of the state apparatus and frequently provided intelligence to the "Red Orchestra," the most successful spy network in occupied Europe, were of immense assistance to the Russians.

Why there weren't any mutinies among the German Army's rank and file even after the string of setbacks that started with Stalingrad in 1943 calls for some explanation. The Eastern Front ought to have been a prime location for uprising. The idea of the master race had been deeply ingrained in the minds of German warriors. In the Soviet Union, the Wehrmacht committed atrocities against Jews and Slavs that were comparable to those committed by the SS. Mass rapes, the execution of Soviet POWs, and the invasion's barbarism have all been well documented. Vasily Grossman never tried to clean up what he observed in his dispatches from the front lines. He recalled how the Germans treated people, even peasants from the Soviet Union, like animals.

It was too late by 1944. A separate agreement would not have been contemplated by either Roosevelt or Churchill, as was made clear in response to the Germans' feeler-posting. Admiral Wilhelm Canaris, the commander of the Abwehr, started working on a separate peace between Germany and Britain as early as 1941 and again in 1943. He and Sir Stewart Menzies, "C" of MI6, had a strong antipathy to communism in common. They probably believed it was still possible to combine fascism and democracy against the Soviet Union before it was too late. According to circumstantial evidence, the two met face to face in Franco's Spain, a place of safety. However, Kim Philby, the Soviet intelligence operator implanted with British intelligence, thwarted their efforts. The paperwork is alleged to have been frozen by Philby. Whatever Menzies' intentions, there is no proof that the British military high command or Churchill and his war council supported surrender.

Churchill continued to be very dubious about the existence of any significant "internal resistance" to Hitler. He couldn't harbor any illusions since newsreel footage of the actual mass celebrations that followed early Nazi wins was still too fresh in his memory. A separate peace negotiated by Britain and the United States with Canaris and Goering would have been perceived as what it was: a betrayal and a capitulation after the triumphs of the Red Army in 1943 and 1944. A civil war in France and Italy would have been unavoidable, even without anything else.

France's resistance to the Nazis during the war was a convoluted and opaque enterprise. The mythologies that eventually developed around it—stories that most French citizens recognized were made up but that were nevertheless viewed as important to preserve the "honor" of France—made the mixture of lies and cover-ups even more egregious. The Resistance narrative had two main iterations. In essence, both internal and external forces were used to establish the Resistance. The British SOE organized the external resistance with the help of General de Gaulle's eccentric group of patriotic nationalists, extreme monarchists, and well-intentioned uniformed hangers-on. The latter were represented locally in the internal resistance, together with communists (after June 1941) and leftist sympathizers who were mostly located in the workplaces and underground cells.

De Gaulle was held up by the Gaullists as the embodiment of France. The General himself started the post-war era with the blatant lie that France had been "liberated by herself, by her own people with the help of the armies of France, with the support and aid of the entire France, of fighting France, of the only France, of the true France, of the eternal France." This significantly underplayed the support offered to Hitler by the men and women of Vichy, in addition to neglecting the roles of Britain and the United States. How about Vichy? They were dismissed with an obnoxious hand wave: "quelques malheureux traîtres," or "a few unfortunate traitors." The majority of France was fully aware of how absurd this hallucinogenic idea was.

Such films were made feasible by the 1968 political and cultural revolutions in France (as well as Germany, Italy, and Japan). The movie was completed over three years after it was first released because the public broadcaster ORTF refused to air it. The majority of French people have not seen it as of yet.

The ethically dubious writings of novelist Patrick Modiano, who also co-wrote Louis Malle's lackluster attempt with Lucien Lacombe and was criticized by reviewer Serge Dany for missing any social and political context, however, presented a challenge to the film's clarity. It was not surprising that Modiano gained the respect of many collaborators or that a former close adviser of Pierre Laval gave him the literary award he got (in May 1968!). In nations like Italy, Greece, and the former Yugoslavia, the idea of the occupied era as an intractable problem is currently becoming more popular. Many, especially political traitors whose illusions in Stalin had been deceived, were driven by the urge to cloak the communist struggle and bury it in the sea.

What did Churchill think of de Gaulle and his group, who were now living in London and acting like the French government? In some ways, the two guys resembled each other. The first was a politician who enjoyed playing soldiers and frequently irritated people who were on the receiving end of his meddling in military issues. The other was a soldier by birth and bred, but his decision to get involved in politics right after the war (and ultimately to overthrow the Fourth Republic) was not as well received as he would have liked.

Wherever he could, Churchill cherished the concept of reinstating monarchs. It was impossible to do so in France, but after closely observing de Gaulle, he knew le General was the finest alternative. Churchill gave Europe's colonial empires top importance, as I have stated numerous times, and their post-war stability had to be maintained even if the final cost was the organization of a seamless transfer of the empires from Europe to the United States. For this reason, Roosevelt and Churchill contemplated seriously imposing two mild-mannered French colonialists in North Africa — Admiral Darlan and General Giraud — whom they had managed to wrest from Vichy.

De Gaulle developed his own ideas on the post-war system as a result of the same experience: France and French sovereignty, not Washington or Moscow. He later removed France from NATO for this reason. One of the main Gaullist tenets was the defense of French imperial interests. The vast majority of those who have made de Gaulle into a giraffe god are now opposed to these same principles. The defining characteristics of modern France include praise for de Gaulle, Atlanticism, and acceptance of the German economic Anschluss. According to Wikileaks, when Chirac refused to support the Iraq war in 2003, his socialist rival Françoise Hollande hurried to the US embassy to tell the ambassador that this would not have happened if he had been president.

Thus, this is the result of 1944. De Gaulle, Churchill, and Roosevelt concurred that the majority of Vichy's servants, including the army, police, courts, and imprisoned technicians, should remain a part of the "Liberation." De Gaulle had Pétain tried and sentenced to death, but this was reduced to life in prison (he spent the remainder of his life on a benighted prison-island, a French specialty). Pétain had been sentenced to death in absentia by De Gaulle.

President Mitterrand, who had served as a Vichy employee in the early stages of the war, paid a visit to Pétain's mausoleum in 1992. It is up for debate as to whether he did it as an act of reconciliation or to rekindle the camaraderie of his youth.

It is unfortunate that the French Resistance was never able to find a historian with the skills of Claudio Pavone, whose massive work on the Italian Resistance continues to dominate that nation's historiography on the subject, despite Berlusconi, Meloni, and Salvini's gradual restoration of Mussolini.

The king and key military authorities, including Marshal Bagdolio, started talking about getting rid of Mussolini and offering the Allies a peace pact in 1943, sort of like a Vichy in reverse. Dissension from below was present at the same time. Workers at the Turin Rasetti factory went on strike on March 5. Workers from nine more plants joined them two days later. By the end of the month, the city had essentially come to a halt. The political birthplace of Gramsci was once more vibrant. Four months later, the Allies landed in Sicily as the strikes continued to spread beyond city limits and impact numerous additional northern towns.

Vittorio Emanuele III realized he needed to quickly distance himself from Mussolini if he wanted to survive. The Fascist Grand Council gathered on July 24, not long after Rome had been attacked for the first time, and they approved a motion that was critical of Mussolini. The following day, when Il Duce went to see the king, he was confronted, demanded to resign, and taken into custody by armed guards.

Large-scale Italian partisan resistance against the Nazi occupation began after the Allies and Nazis signed an armistice in September 1943. By April 1945, there were over 100,000 members, of which 35,000 were dead. The Anglo-American armies, with the Resistance forces serving as a critical auxiliary, defeated Mussolini and the fascist regime he represented. At Yalta, it was decided that the fascist and proto-fascist countries of Italy and France would belong to the West, or the United States. That the Marseillaise was engraved on the hearts of those who sang Marechal, nous voila. While there was compliance, resignation, fear, despair, self-interest, betrayal, and shame, Carmen Callil suggested in Bad Faith, her illuminating biography of Louis Darquier, Vichy's "Commissioner for Jewish Affairs," that "a strong sense of sullen, hungry fury growls through these years of the new French Fatherland."

De Gasperi was viewed by Truman and Churchill as the prototypical anti-communist. He easily outsmarted his PCI competitor Palmiro Togliatti thanks to his political savvy, intelligence, and tact. A Gramsci was what the PCI was in need of. Instead, they received a Comintern apparatchik who oversaw the organization, together with a group of Stalinist MPs. Togliatti was neither a wise politician nor a profound theorist. He had revealed his true self as a cynical, cold-blooded operative who followed orders throughout the Spanish Civil War. In 1944, when he traveled from Moscow to Rome, he made it obvious that a revolution was not in the cards and gave the Resistance the go-ahead to disarm.

Churchill and Truman intentionally misunderstood the Soviet Union's policy when they defended the old-new structures of the Italian state on the grounds that the Soviet Union's wrath and cleverness should never be underestimated. Churchill had related to his doctor, Lord Moran, how Stalin once turned to him after dinner in the Kremlin flat in 1942 and inquired as to why he feared Russia. The Soviet Union had no desire to take over the entire planet. Churchill mumbled incoherently that he remembered having a similar discussion with Ribbentrop. Moscow never contested the pre-Yalta agreement that the US would control Italy and that the British could do whatever they pleased in Greece, and the two communist parties in both nations upheld it. One may even argue that the severity of the communist danger was inversely correlated with the anti-communist excesses, as Eric Hobsbawm previously noted. The political appeal of the local parties was minimal in Germany and the USA, the two democracies that restricted or outlawed the legality of communist parties.

Chapter 12:
The Origins of the Cold War: Yugoslavia, Greece, Spain

Churchill contemplated carefully how to prevent the Greek Resistance, which was predominately communist, from assuming too much power. The same is true of Yugoslavia. His preferred option was to restore the monarchies in both nations.

Churchill was in a good mood because he was happy that he had gotten his way. After a few drinks, he addressed Stalin, saying, "It's a shame God didn't ask our opinion when he created the world." 'That was God's first error,' the Georgian said. Did the two thieves chuckle and crack open a new bottle? Very likely. Whatever the reason, NATO had abandoned the Greek people, which led to a civil war after the Second World War and, later, a brutal military dictatorship.

Stalin agreed to a partition of "spheres" in Europe at Yalta in 1945 and promised not to meddle in Italy or France, where the two communist parties had become mass parties as a result of the resistance they had commanded and the amazing military victories of the Red Army. The Yalta agreement's true intent has frequently been misunderstood, with Western ideologues frequently characterizing it as a necessary Stalinist capitulation. This is deceptive. Always a two-edged sword, Yalta. In addition to approving Soviet control of Eastern Europe, this act also authorized a powerful and hegemonic US presence in Western Europe. This presence was crucial for the creation of NATO, and it was strengthened by what appear to be permanent US military bases in Germany, Italy, and Britain. Finally, the development of nuclear weapons systems and their deployment in Western Europe added to this hegemony.

According to the piece of paper, Greece should be a part of the Western domain, and Yugoslavia should be split equally between the US/Britain and the Soviet Union. It was a poorly thought-out scheme. not the only one, though. Roosevelt and Churchill also talked about the circumstances under which the Soviet Union may join the war against Japan in Yalta. All three commanders concurred that Russia would be given a sphere of influence in Manchuria following Japan's capitulation in exchange for Soviet involvement in the Pacific theater. This would include a portion of Sakhalin, the Kuril Islands, a lease at Port Arthur, and a stake in running the Manchurian railroads. They were obviously not paying close attention to what was happening in China. Events in Yugoslavia and Greece provided evidence that decisions made at the top table are not always embraced by those seated below. The experience in the Balkans served as a sobering reminder of this fact.

On April 6, 1941, at 2.30 a.m., the Yugoslav ambassador signed a friendship treaty with Moscow in hopes that it would prevent a German invasion while the Stalin-Hitler treaty was still in force. It wasn't to be. A little while afterwards, the Luftwaffe breached Yugoslav airspace by taking off from Bulgarian airfields and bombarding Belgrade nonstop and heavily. The Wehrmacht moved to capture Zagreb at the same time it crossed the Austrian-Slovenian border at Maribor. The Second German Army arrived in Belgrade on April 8. Italian, Hungarian, and Bulgarian soldiers invaded the nation on April 10 and tore it apart as Hitler had intended.

Here, the Stalin-Hitler Pact rendered the party Moscow's puppet partially paralyzed, preventing it from even waging sabotage against the occupiers. Ethnically a Croat, Tito vowed to reunite Yugoslavia and refused to accept the division of his nation. He also criticized the fascist state that the Third Reich had established in Croatia. On May 8, 1941, Moscow acknowledged that the Axis had divided up Yugoslavia. After advising the ambassador that there was no longer a legal foundation for a Yugoslav mission in Moscow, they expelled him.

The communist parties of Greece and Yugoslavia respectively led the two resistance movements in the Balkans that made an impression on the Allies. In the latter instance, the majority of SOE observers on the ground or special envoys dispatched to evaluate Tito, like Fitzroy MacLean, were impressed by the Croat communists and horrified by the alternative. The Croat nationalists, known as the Ustashe, were commanded by men who openly and joyfully collaborated with Hitler and were fascists. They provided armed militias to fight Tito's multiethnic guerrilla army. The Chetniks in Serbia did not openly cooperate, but their enmity for Tito was on par with the Ustashe. There was no other course of action that a reasonable British presence in Yugoslavia could have recommended than arming and supplying Tito's forces. Randolph Churchill, who had been dropped into the nation by parachute, was also impressed by the communist-led resistance. The novelist Evelyn Waugh was the lone contrarian, viewing Tito's early distaste as an irrational prejudice rather than a philosophical judgment of a quality for which he was already well-known.

What led the British to support Tito? The strategic choice was made as a result of the 1942 Axis defection of the commanders of the Serbian Chetnik movement. Only the Chetniks were capable of successfully disrupting enemy communications at that time. Instead, they started assisting the Germans. Churchill responded indignantly. When all attempts at persuasion and enticement had failed, Hitler first curtailed the weapons' supply to them before deciding to stop all future shipments in 1943.

Because Dimitrov supported him as the leader of Yugoslavia who could be relied upon, Tito was able to survive his trips to Moscow. He kept a very low profile, shunned pointless interactions, and avoided minor intrigues. Stalin was once observed by him viewing the Comintern meetings from behind a pillar. Nothing further. He never requested a meeting with him or met him. Later, when an independent Yugoslavia and its leaders made it plain that they would not be used as Stalin's puppet, the real conflicts began.

Stalin and Churchill's feeble attempts to persuade Tito to agree to King Peter's restoration as the titular head were graciously denied. Churchill did not stir up any trouble. For the British Empire, Yugoslavia had no strategic significance. The key to Tito's victory was the multi-ethnic nature of the Communist Party he led and the Resistance it produced, which brought together intellectuals and workers to fight fascism. The only force able to do this was its own. The Third Reich was openly and voluntarily partnered with Chetnik, Ustashe, and some Bosniak detachments.

Tito went all-out for a socialist revolution in defiance of Stalin's orders. Following this judgment, there was a rise in confidence and public support. Tito warned Stalin that any attempt to overthrow the Yugoslav government would be met with resistance after the Soviet leader promised punishment. The populace of Yugoslavia would be armed. Tito was chased out of the global communist movement for this "crime." The stigma served as a badge of honor for him. Normalcy wasn't reestablished until after Stalin's demise.

The Admiralty and the political class continued to accept this even though it had been stated decades earlier when it came to formulating strategy and tactics starting in 1942. Crowe's statements helped to explain Churchill's infatuation with Greece and his merciless drive to seize power there, despite the tremendous cost in material resources and human life. This was combined with his own naval fixation. One of the best perspectives of imperialist banditry in action was to be provided by it.

Many SOE operatives in the nation were aware that the Resistance's political fecklessness had made it possible for the British to invade after the Germans left. C. M. Woodhouse, an SOE officer, stated unequivocally: "I have no doubt whatsoever that ELAS [the National Popular Liberation Army] could have taken Athens." A British landing would have been very challenging as a result. With the cooperation of a semi-fascist right that had supported the monarchical Metaxas regime from 1936 to 1940 and frequently deploying security battalions that had assisted in policing the Nazi occupation, the British involvement in Greece was intended to first block and then crush the Resistance. The crime committed here was extremely serious. In one of the deadliest periods of the war, Churchill and the British Army put an end to the most effective anti-Nazi Resistance in Europe.

Greece became involved in the Greek Civil War when Churchill was given permission by Stalin to utilize Greece as part of Britain's "sphere of influence." The issue was that, aside from the collaborators, the majority of Greeks were opposed to this approach. Few unbiased observers at the time questioned that Greece belonged to the left because the communist-led Resistance had a significant hand in annoying and rebuffing the German Army. Churchill made the decision to rule out this scenario.

Older Greeks still view Churchill as a tyrant and a murderer because of his pivotal role in the rape of their nation. It in no way mitigates his role since his principal collaborators in this atrocity were his wartime Labour lieutenants Clement Attlee and Ernest Bevin (who perpetrated the program after 1945).

In a contentious discussion at the Labour Party Conference in December 1944, Bevin vigorously backed Churchill. He had been unable to respond to Labour MPs and delegates who were outraged by what their country was doing to Greece in a befuddled, mendacious, and ignorant speech. When Aneurin Bevan, who had been allowed five minutes to speak, told the conference that "only three bodies of public opinion in the world have gone on record in his [Churchill's] support, namely fascist Spain, fascist Portugal, and the majority of the Tories in the House of Commons," he was greeted with thunderous applause. The block vote's trade union wielders were unimpressed. They supported Bevin, the forelock-tugger. Thus, the Labour Party Conference supported Churchill's terror in Greece with the addition of another body (its own).

Several people in the SOE, British intelligence, and the army at the time felt humiliated by the British atrocities in Greece. There were far too many people present who didn't say anything despite being embarrassed and incensed by what was happening. The Times' animosity particularly incensed Churchill, who screamed against the publication in the House of Commons. Robert Barrington-Ward, the editor, was someone he knew well, but he was unable to persuade him to modify his position. In a heated Commons discussion in December 1944, a few Labour MPs pushed back against the government, putting Churchill and his successor Anthony Eden on the defensive—to little avail.

Annan adds that he has no support for American policies or the "detestable colonels who imprisoned some of my Greek friends when they came to power," just in case he has been misinterpreted. In that case, one would wonder why he initially turned over control of Greece to the Americans. The crumbling British Empire was under no obligation to terrorize Greece once the Germans were defeated. Because the British officers who risked their lives in the war "were so traduced," Annan was incensed. The shows criticized the actions of the British officers in Greece, not "in the war." It is clear that they were following Churchill and Scobie's orders, but as the Nuremberg trial would rule a year later, "obeying orders" should no longer be a defense accepted by any court in the future.

All parties might agree on this. Simply put, Churchill was committed to handing the Greeks a defeat that would serve as a lesson to them and to anybody else who might harbor similar thoughts. His way of thought was typical: without a British triumph in Greece, there could be no peace. Pure banditry, that is.

The communist-led Greek Resistance engaged in guerilla warfare and mass mobilizations against the occupying German Army throughout the years 1942 and 1943. The Germans were forced by two general strikes in Athens and Piraeus in April and September 1942 to raise pay and salaries, erect soup kitchens for workers, and declare publicly that no food would be shipped from Greece. Passive opposition to the shipment of Greek "slave labor" to Germany also existed. Every Greek who might have ended up working in German factories turned dumb, deaf, or illiterate when questioned. Greeks were forcibly relocated, but their number was significantly smaller than that of the other subjugated nations.

The decision to bring the monarch back had been approved by Churchill. Roosevelt agreed, but he was unsure. The scene was set for the British Army to seize control of Athens and carry out a brutal crackdown. This operation's criminal nature was well recognized, and it served as the start of the Cold War as we know it today. That explains why Lord Annan and others were so sensitive forty years later. Too much blood was on the hands of Churchill and the British politico-military elite.

Three Tory prime ministers—Churchill, Eden, and Macmillan—excused the bloodshed in Greece a few years after the Red Army's astonishing triumphs against the Third Reich by justification of the conflict as one against "communist bandits."

However, it wasn't just the Tories who delighted in Greece's plight. The statement from Ernest Bevin, the incoming Labour foreign secretary, was sent to the British ambassador in Athens the day after Churchill lost the 1945 election: "There will be no change of policy." Bevin made no apologies for the fact that he was an Empire supporter from birth. He frequently expressed his respect for the British Empire. After Labour took office, all of the left's ambitions in Greece were dashed in under twenty-four hours.

Without an effective alternative to the right-wing regimes imposed or completely supported by NATO, Greece was left without one. Left-wing lawmakers were threatened or murdered, as was the case with prominent Greek deputy Grigoris Lambrakis, who gained notoriety thanks to Z, Costa-Gavras' visually stunning debut picture that astounded younger audiences. The daily repression that many Greeks came to accept as part of existence was added to Churchill's crimes.

The NATO-supported military coup in 1967 was intended to prevent the election of any Greek government that offered even a slight challenge to the existing political and ideological structures of the Churchill-Scobie state. It was based on the atrocities committed by Greek fascists and the army after World War II. The end result was a cruel administration that reopened island prisons, engaged in widespread torture, jailed the renowned Greek composer Mikis Theodorakis and many other people, and drove many intellectuals and students out of the country.

Churchill continued to back Franco both during and after World War II, maintaining him in power in the early post-war years almost entirely on his own. Churchill's decisions in this instance, as in the case of Greece, were influenced by what he saw as British interests, his support for fascism against "international Jews and communists," and his refusal to accept counsel to the contrary from within the establishment. He was aware of the support for the Spanish Republic in Britain. For instance, hundreds of workers in London protested a British Union of Fascists gathering in Cable Street in the east of the city in October 1936 despite warnings from the government and orders from the Labour Party. This kind of anti-fascist effort was what caused the left-liberal and Marxist elite to grow rapidly before 1939. The pacifists among them were scorned and reviled by Churchill, but he would need them as the war approached.

The "English Quisling" prepared a brief book, Ambassador on Special Mission, upon his return to London in 1945, stating to the Foreign Office that "my object is to make the complete case against Franco as soon as possible." Churchill and his friends responded, "No dice, old boy." Ernest Bevin, Labour's foreign secretary, gave a similar reaction. Hoare, a former appeaser like Churchill, had grown to despise Franco and the Falangists.

While the official stance of Great Britain and the United States was one of "cold reserve," Counselor R. J. Bowker observed on June 12 in a dispatch from the Madrid embassy that "General Franco knows that neither power is going to use force to turn him out." While this is going on, there are significant business exchanges with both Powers, and there are promising signs for the development of post-war economic connections that will be advantageous to all three parties.

Churchill and Roosevelt were adamant the Soviet Union was the enemy of the future during the entire conflict. US policy had been this since Woodrow Wilson. Hitler wasn't able to do what Churchill had anticipated he would for the West. The Soviet Union's contribution to the war's victory had given it true popularity in the West. It took some time, but the West, led by the US, persisted in changing this perception. When necessary, Churchill was more than willing to be wheeled onto the stage.

Churchill's circumstances prevented him from taking more drastic action. Acheson later recounts his annoyance at "the apparent sincerity with which, until almost the end of the war, the neutrals and British alike voiced fear of German occupation to justify trade with the enemy" in his memoirs of the conflict.

Churchill had long made it known that he would choose Franco over the elected republican leaders if given the chance. He authorized the spending of $10 million during the war to bribe Franco's generals in exchange for their vow to prevent their leader from entirely siding with the Axis forces. Captain Alan Hillgarth, the British naval attaché, who served as the Iberian peninsula's chief of intelligence and counterintelligence, was given control of the operation.

For at least a year, it was intended to keep Franco from becoming "belligerent." On the surface, it seemed to have succeeded, but a turning point was reached when Hitler refused to give in to Franco's colonial lust in order to alienate Pétain and Vichy. The Spanish dictator would have given in and followed orders if the war had gone well for the Third Reich, but after the Soviet successes at Stalingrad and Kursk, his sense of self-preservation kicked in. Franco withdrew the 20,000-man Blue Division in 1943 on Churchill's recommendation, despite the fact that thousands of Spaniards had already died and hundreds were held as prisoners of war in the Soviet Union. Given their political views, a number of thousand of them refused to go back and naturally joined the Waffen SS.

Roosevelt felt uncomfortable with Franco being in the Western camp. In order to force through some superficial reforms, Churchill significantly softened his stance and said he may accept a pro-Western administration as long as the monarchy was reinstated and a Bourbon was placed back on the throne. Democracy played a very minor role in all of this. Without much trouble, Franco outwitted the elderly guy in Downing Street. From 1939 to 1975, when Franco was in power, there would be no monarchy; King Juan Carlos would be his replacement. Churchill repressed his irritation. Rejection of NATO membership was viewed as a rap on the back. Franco didn't seem to care. In most cases, Churchill favoured a supplicant king and a far-right government.

The Moncloa Pacts, which symbolized the 'democratic rupture' after Franco's death, were put into effect by the Spanish government in 1976. Legalizing political parties and trade unions was undoubtedly a blow to some parts of the Spanish bourgeoisie, who preferred a dictatorship. Due to a "state of exception," Spanish capitalism had been growing for over forty years and had flourished during the last fifteen years of the Franco administration. The 'economic miracle' that led to growth rates akin to Japan during that time was fueled by the repression of the working class. From 1964 to 1971, there was a notable increase. Because of Franco, Spanish industrialists only lost twenty to twenty-five minutes of labor per employee annually as a result of strikes. The administration had banned working-class opposition and imprisoned all dissenters for forty years, sending armed police into the industries to beat and jail strikers. Spanish capitalism required free trade unions with which to communicate in order to justify its economic dominance under a new political rule. However, they continued to hold onto other privileges from the past, some of which hardly belong in a fully-fledged bourgeois democracy.

Chapter 13:
The East Is Dead, the East Is Red: Japan, China, Korea, Vietnam

Officially, the Second World War came to an end in Asia, where it had started. With Truman's decision to test the newly developed atomic bomb on Hiroshima and Nagasaki, what had begun with what appeared to be a minor armed conflict between Japan and China on the Marco Polo Bridge outside of Beijing, came to an inconceivable end. A global trend led to the transfer of European and Japanese colonies in Asia to the United States. In contrast to Europe, where the Yalta agreement was implemented by all parties (with the exception of Yugoslavia), opposition throughout Asia resulted in new liberation battles.

In his cool reply, Roosevelt clarified that he was referring about "enemy possessions." Churchill reluctantly agreed to this, however these so-called "possessions" were actually post-1918 League of Nations mandates. Though this was never carried out, it was agreed that the UN, which was just about to be created, might inspect and meddle in British-controlled territory. Churchill insisted that the French should prevent Vietnam from gaining independence and offered them complete support. In 1945, Ho Chi Minh had already proclaimed the nation independent, and massive public mobilizations had greeted the occasion. But that was not to be. With the support of the British, the French began their colonial conflict; in 1954, the United States seized over and continued it until 1975.

The fact that Churchill, Attlee, and Stalin all supported the nuclear attacks does not excuse the United States. The bomb was constructed, tested, Oppenheimer chose a fitting passage from Hindu scriptures to convey some reservations, the pilots followed instructions, and they watched the mushroom cloud form. Was the stunned apathy shown at the time by Western populations merely another illustration of the strong hold that imperialist ideology exercises with its ingrained racism and civilizational death wish.

The level of animosity toward Japanese people in the US peaked to the point where majority Americans approved of the internment of Japanese-Americans during the war, despite the fact that many of them were engaged in combat with people of similar ethnic backgrounds in the US Army. I doubt there would have been many objections if the US had decided to take similar action against Muslim Americans in the wake of 9/11. There was a time when so many pundits were making the parallel between 9/11 and Pearl Harbor that it made many Muslim Americans terrified. In order to emphasize that the Middle East wars were a Muslim problem and had little to do with US/EU foreign policy, the constant junior ally

Britain institutionalized espionage on Muslims in schools, colleges, and at home. It says a lot that isn't frequently spoken in public that censorship and monitoring are now state policies in Britain and are supported by all three parties in Parliament.

Imperialist states have typically been characterized by their refusal to take any responsibility for war and damage. Additionally, as John W. Dower demonstrates in his sober and thorough analysis of race in the Pacific War, perceptions of the Japanese as a people had always been qualified in some way. In an effort to dehumanize and mystify the Japanese, weaponized psychobabble was used against them. What you are unable to comprehend must be inferior. During the Second World War, a lot of this kind of content was used frequently in US and Western propaganda.

The extent and crudeness of anti-Japanese racism in the United States and Britain astounded steadfast champions of China against the Japanese occupation and crimes, such as Pearl Buck and Lin Yutang, who anticipated a conflict between the white and non-white worlds within a generation. What they did not expect was how hard right-wing and liberal Japanese politicians would work to defeat the Japanese left, establish an effective one-party state, learn to love baseball and Hollywood movies, and become 'normal' just like the people of the West, under the guidance of their divine emperor and with their nation permanently occupied by US troops. That was all there was to it. The atomic bombs were said to have cleared the field. Old malignancies have all vanished. Only careful control was required. If Japanese officials did not comply with the White House's demands, the US base in Okinawa was the last resort, a condition that still exists today.

Following the conquering of Japan, US officials' focus switched to the entire region, where the groundwork for national upheavals in Vietnam and Korea—colonial territories of France and Japan, respectively—was being laid. Local communists had organized resistance movements against the Japanese in both nations. More concerning for the United States and its allies was the impending resumption of a civil war in China, where the Chinese Communist Party was also gaining ground. The stars had spoken of a revolution.

Korea had previously been a Japanese protectorate and, later, a full-fledged colony. Churchill and Truman were unprepared for the circumstances that resulted from Japan's defeat in 1945. Communists were mostly in charge of the subsequent nationalist resistance in all of the former Japanese colonial possessions in the area. Due to widespread desertions to Mao Zedong's army, the Guomindang (GMD) in China suffered such severe wounds from its ambiguous stance toward the Japanese that the civil war tended to be quite one-sided. Thus, it became inevitable that the Chinese Revolution would occur.

Chiang Kai-shek and his GMD were backed by Churchill, Roosevelt, and Truman as the only genuine answer for China. Arms for the GMD soldiers poured down the Burma Road from the US and Britain. He was accompanied to various international gatherings, and a seat on the Security Council of the incoming United Nations had been offered to his China. Churchill thought of Chiang as the de Gaulle of China.

There is little doubt that a communist revolution would have been imminent in Korea if the US had abandoned the country. The Korean Communist Party was the biggest political force in the nation after Japan's defeat, as Bruce Cumings has maintained in two books and several essays over the years. In addition to everything else, at least 100,000 Koreans had fought alongside the Chinese Red Armies in China against the Japanese. A handful of them had earlier enlisted in Mao's Long March to the outpost in Yenan. The native Korean forces—those organizations that had remained loyal to the Japanese for many years—were not powerful enough to thwart the revolution, which was commonly referred to in that era's Western jargon as "Soviet expansionism." This was understood by American policymakers.

Stalin just made yet another terrible error. He consented to Truman's proposal to let US soldiers occupy the southern portion of the peninsula because the Red Army was practically within walking distance of Pusan. Why? The US had argued that they should be the only ones in control of Japan. All the Soviet Union had to do was allow communists in Korea to establish a government that, unlike some of the Allied constructs in eastern Europe, would have widespread support. The 'Soviet expansionists' were responsible for allowing the United States to invade Korea and establishing the stage for the ensuing three-year conflict. Stalin had disastrously misjudged Hitler, Churchill, and Truman, in that order.

In Korea, the US was stalemated, but in Vietnam, a Communist Party that battled valiantly and resolutely defeated them. Rarely have two successive Western imperial empires been vanquished by members of the same leadership generation. The French had believed they could put an end to the Vietnamese resistance. They had derisively mocked General Vo Nguyen Giap, calling him a "bush general." They believed they were unbeatable due to their white skin and prior victories. In his very realistic way, Mao Zedong famously said: "In real life we cannot ask for "ever triumphant" generals." Giap enthusiastically concurred, but he was aware that by 1954, morale and battle spirit in his National Liberation Army had peaked. Later, he would clarify that the role the Vietnamese Communist Party had played in 1945 was a factor in the support it had attracted.

The biggest protest movement in American history was started by the Vietnamese people's refusal to submit to defeat, and it spread to the soldiers as well. The National Liberation Front's tanks reached Saigon in April 1975. Helicopters were used to flee by US personnel and a few hangers-on. It was the first time ever that the United States had been so thoroughly defeated. Kabul in August 2021 resembled it, but it had a distinct design.

The 1960s European uprising opened the door for discussion and criticism of the way the Second World War and its aftermath had been portrayed. The most obvious indication that sizable elements of the new generation were repulsed by the failure to make amends with fascism was the emergence of urban terrorist organizations in three Axis countries, Germany, Italy, and Japan.

Chapter 14:
Castles in the Sand: Re-mapping the Arab East

Not all historical facts can stand on their own. They are frequently overlooked or misunderstood. even more so in this century. For example, it is critical to recognize that the past holds the key to understanding the present in the Arab East. The Middle East has become the focus of a persistent military engagement by the United States and its allies, and the remapping of the region is still ongoing. We need to go back to Churchill's early imperial years to understand why.

Churchill oversaw 100,000 British and Indian soldiers in Mesopotamia while serving as secretary of state for war. Churchill sought a quick handover of Egypt's partial autonomy to the British Empire even though it had existed under the Ottoman era. Nationalists from Egypt violently protested. In Cairo, there were open demonstrations. The colonial secretary and ardent imperialist Alfred Milner said in 1920 that the Ottoman agreement with Egypt was not a bad idea, and that the British should just put on Ottoman clothing and footwear and continue as before.

Although Egyptian nationalists sought a significant degree of independence, Britain was able to secure everything it sought through negotiations, including complete military control over the Suez Canal region, defense, and the protection of foreign interests. Sudan was designated as the country that Britain would "protect," and if there was any doubt, Egypt's foreign policy would be bound to that of the UK. Churchill had absolutely no reason to complain, yet he did. He detested the idea of bargaining with the Egyptians in order to win the approval of an oppressed elite. He threw another temper tantrum, promising anyone who would listen that he would "fight to the end." He voted in favor of the Allenby Plan four days after accepting the Cabinet's decision.

Churchill was most concerned that Indian nationalists would be inspired to demand the same, which would pose a challenge to the Empire. As we've seen, his capacity for strategic thought was lacking. He was given his own space to complete further readjustments in the area. The French received Syria from the San Remo Conference in 1920, while the remaining former Ottoman provinces went to Britain. Mesopotamia came first on Churchill's list, followed by Palestine and Transjordan. No one was to be called to a meeting, much less a negotiation, not even the notables.

Churchill agreed in full. He would have laughed if he had read her letters to her father and stepmother, in which she effortlessly transitioned from the new dresses in the Harvey Nichols catalog to the need for using chemical weapons against the rebellious Kurds. Three former Ottoman provinces—Baghdad, Basra, and Mosul—were haphazardly tied together at the creation of the new state of Iraq, with Kuwait being broken off as a separate principality. Mosul was in complete violation of the armistice agreements. Bell's idea for total British domination via an Arab smokescreen received the strong support of Curzon.

Churchill hurriedly dismissed the India Office's concerns about chemical warfare by asserting that "Gas is a more merciful weapon than high explosive shell and compels an enemy to accept a decision with less loss of life." In Wiltshire, the Porton Down Lab was founded in 1916 specifically for the aim of conducting experiments in biological and chemical warfare.

Unsurprisingly, the sentiment was anti-British and expanded to other parts of the nation. Sir Percy Cox, Gertrude Bell's supervisor, had told the Basra residents that the British would arrive "as liberators not conquerors" in 1914. Regardless of their religious affiliation, the majority of people saw the British as intruders, and participation in covert anti-colonial organisations, both Sunni and Shia, skyrocketed after a monarchy was imposed.

The newly formed League of Nations described the post-First World War states to be formed from former German, Ottoman, and Austro-Hungarian possessions as either "advanced nations" (white populations) or nations "that could not yet stand up for themselves" (non-white populations) and thus required imperialist tutelage. The latter group was further divided into those who were closest to self-rule and those who were most removed. The 'top' category in the Middle East included Palestine, Syria, Lebanon, and Iraq; as a result, these governments were identified as eventual recipients of self-rule. According to this statement, Palestine was a functional province rather than a "empty land." These states would be controlled by Mandates from the League granted to Britain and France until self-rule was established.

Churchill was a strong supporter of a Jewish homeland, but even before he was born, the seventh Earl of Shaftesbury, an Evangelical Christian, initiated the process of deporting European Jews to Palestine in 1838. He suggested this to Palmerston, the then-foreign secretary, in order to ensure Great Power protection. Pieties from the Old Testament were combined with British strategic requirements. Speaking to Parliament a few decades later, Shaftesbury provided another justification for why a new British colony was practically essential for the Empire, contributing to the idea that the lands were depopulated:

In 1919, Balfour told his cabinet members that there was no need to waste too much time carrying out the statement that bore his name since "in Palestine we do not propose even to go through the form of consulting the wishes of the present inhabitants." Since "all the four Great powers are committed to Zionism," there was no need for this. This was much more important than what the 700,000 Arabs wanted and thought. Churchill emphasized this even more by equating Palestinian Arabs with Australian Aboriginals and Native Americans.

This is the voice of white supremacy, a viewpoint that was reaffirmed more than 50 years later by Benny Morris, Israel's leading revisionist historian and a former paratrooper. Such an admission of the long-denied crimes and atrocities done against the Palestinians in 1948 during the "War of Independence" would have thrilled Churchill. This sums up Churchill's personal beliefs as well as

Jewish Israel's common sense from top to bottom and the Balfour Declaration's final rationale.

Churchill didn't write a lot about his own views on Zionism and Jews in general. However, it is evident from what he did write that his opinions on Israel's founding were not always consistent. His justifications ranged from blatant instrumentalism (it would benefit the British Empire in an area populated by Arab adversaries) to racism based on civilisation and anti-Bolshevism.

Churchill had to have sufficient knowledge of English history. Why was it not mentioned that England had started the worst pogroms and persecution of Jews in ancient Europe? The fact that Henry III had issued a royal decree known as "The Edict of the Badge" in 1218 that required Jews to wear a "marking badge" would have pleased German fascists. Sixty years later, thieving baron-led pogroms resulted in the murder of over a thousand Jews, including 500 in London. Edward I issued the 'Edict of Expulsion' in 1290. The property of the Jews was plundered, and the blood-libel accusation was propagated with a zeal that Goebbels would have envied. All Jews were picked up and exiled. This is a perfect example of the adage "past is prologue." A few Jews escaped to France. Others found safety in Muslim Spain, where sizable, free Jewish communities actively participated in state affairs at all levels.

The First World War served as the prelude to the 1953 Anglo-American revolution in Iran, which overthrew the popular nationalist, liberal-democratic prime leader Mohammed Mossadegh (nicknamed "Messy Duck" in Churchill's pathetic remark).

On Curzon's instructions, Sir Percy Cox, the British minister in Tehran, entered into secret negotiations with Vosuq and two of his close associates not long after the infamous Treaty of Versailles approved the continuation of European colonialism by rejecting any demand for national self-determination from colonized peoples. A new covert pact that practically turned Iran into a protectorate of Britain was the goal.16 Vosuq agreed to the transaction as long as the British paid the three of them a consulting fee and related expenses. A verbal invoice for 500,000 tomans was presented to the

British. Mohammed Mossadegh, a dissident Majlis (Parliament) member, calculated the figures to be the equivalent of £131,000 at the time. The money was paid, and the arrangement was completed in 1919 with the appointment of British "advisers" to oversee the treasury and the army.

Others in London were also very active. Churchill, in his capacity as minister of war, opposed Curzon's exploits in this case and joined the India Office in calling for an end to the situation. Churchill even insisted that there should be no resistance when a naval fleet led by veteran Bolshevik Raskolnikov arrived at the Caspian port of Enzili to demand the return of Russian ships moored there. Lord Hardinge, the Viceroy of India, and Churchill were both very concerned that any significant British setback in Iran would have negative effects on India. Hardinge made it obvious that Curzon wouldn't receive any Indian troops in his support.

The Allies started to be concerned about Reza's pro-Axis stance during the Second World War. The British deposed him in 1941 and installed his son in his stead. Reza was exiled to South Africa, where he later passed away. Churchill and Stalin separated the nation for a brief while in order to protect the oil that was deemed essential for the war, but the Red Army quickly retreated after the Allies' triumph in 1945.

Trade, military assistance, and the Anglo-Iranian Oil Company, whose management acted like colonial commanders and had nothing but contempt for Iranian authorities, were all ways that British power was kept in place. The Iranians believed they were being treated unfairly since royalties changed. They asked that the oil shares be split equally, as the US and the Saudis had agreed. The British objected, insistent on maintaining their majority position. Political organizations, both Islamic and secular, reacted vehemently. The Fedayeen-i-Islam killed the pro-British prime minister General Razmara on March 7, 1951. A resolution requesting the nationalization of the oil business was swiftly passed by the Majlis. Street protests forced the Shah to name Mohammed Mossadegh as prime minister when the National Front, a secular constitutionalist party, gained prominence.

After Labour lost the election in 1951, Churchill returned to power and convinced Truman to back a coup against Mossadegh. The assignment was given to the SIS (MI6) and the CIA. It used to be widely accepted that the CIA was the main player. perhaps on paper. However, Churchill was adamant about showing Mossadegh the door for daring to nationalize British assets.

In the near term, the coup proved successful for the West. It had ousted a well-liked prime minister, the nationalist administration, and the Tudeh Party (a communist party). The Shah's supporters as well as his cunning, avaricious, and unscrupulous twin sister smashed the trade union movement. A relatively small public demonstration in favor of the Shah took place. To help expand the audience, the pimps, prostitutes, and thugs of downtown Tehran recruited a few people who were similar to themselves. As a result, a two-bit general named Fazlollah Zahedi became the new prime minister. Kashani and Behbehani, two significant ayatollahs, were persuaded to offer their blessings.

Before leaving as prime minister in 1955, Churchill's last contribution to the cause of "freedom" and "democracy" would be the regime transition in Iran. His own group let out a resounding sigh of relief. It was a little early. Anthony Eden, Churchill's successor, was unable to grasp the crucial lesson of the Iranian coup, which was that such actions could only be effective with US backing. He immediately started working on a plan to overthrow Egypt's government with France and Israel. The United States did not support the 1956 Suez conflict. Washington was furious and demanded a quick pullout. When Gamal Abdel Nasser nationalized the Suez Canal, the Arab world was already electrified. After the Zionist entity and its imperialist friends were expelled by Washington, his standing in the Arab world rose.

Eden was also short-lived. How about the specter in the attic? Churchill did not speak much, but he did write to President Eisenhower to convey his deep concern about the state of the two countries' ties and his hope that they would soon improve. Though the majority of Anglo-American diplomats and politicians already recognized this, the Suez tragedy had only made it public. Churchill's dominion had come to an end. The game was over, but the burial rites would have to wait for another ten years.

Chapter 15:
War Crimes in Kenya

Churchill's final decade and the death spasms of the British Empire are both currently occurring in the developing world. Kenya serves as an example. Its territory was given to European immigrants when it was seized by the British in 1895. The highlands, where the whites first arrived in 1905, had the richest soil. African protesters' animals were taken and sold. By 1910, Europeans were receiving 600 acres a year. They paid only £10 a year for a holding of 5,000 acres while renting the farms and land on 999-year leases. A little more than 2,000 settlers held more than 5 million acres of Kenya by 1930. To cut down on London's import costs, the British government chose to cultivate maize, sisal, and coffee. Sixty days a year were dedicated to beating Africans into performing forced labor. They were relocated from their traditional territory and housed in huts on reservations near the farms. It was the most extreme instance of white exploitation of black people and a sort of compensated slavery.

The colonial powers of Europe faced a dire situation at the end of the Second World War. Their flaws had been exposed by the world war, and they were aware that they were powerless to make any progress without US political and military backing. Churchill was well aware that the British Empire was dependent on US generosity since it had run out of money.

Even the most ardent Labour imperialists recognized they couldn't maintain India once they won the election in 1945. With the exception of Churchill, most Conservatives shared this viewpoint. The end of the war had brought about a change in attitude within India itself. In February 1946, naval ratings in Mumbai staged a coup and took control of the battleships. Together, Hindu and Muslim seamen refused to bargain with the British. Karachi did the same. Admiral Godfrey raged and vowed retaliation in classic Churchillian fashion.

It was merely empty talk. There was a rise in nationalism. In Egypt, Iraq, and Iran, the Churchill-preferred corrupt and ineffective rulers faced grave danger. Names like Kenyatta, Nkrumah, Mboya, Mandela, Nyerere, Nasser, and Ben Bella were starting to appear in the Anglo-American press as British colonies in Africa were seething beneath the surface. The independence of India in 1947, the victory of the Chinese revolution in 1949, and the French defeat at Dien Bien Phu in 1954 all had a significant influence on the growth of the liberation movements in Africa.

This was the product of the colonial mind. Churchill would have agreed with every idea that Eliot presented. Both men held to the idea of a "protective civilization," as they put it. As was his habit, Churchill became involved in the conflicts in Kenya in 1921 between European settlers and more recent Indian settlers who wanted to end racial segregation. He pretended to be reasonable by telling Edwin Montagu, a fellow Cabinet member tasked with mediating the conflict, that he wasn't against desegregation on principle but that the sanitary laws needed to be so strict that few Indians would be able to meet European standards. (I'll refrain from rambling on about the hygienic conditions in Britain in the early 20th century.)

Churchill degrades the colonized in this instance and many others to exalt the colonizer. It is not sufficient to take their lands. It is necessary to cast doubt on their very humanity in order for some of them to develop a sense of inferiority. They must be subjected to such a degree of oppression that the use of force, the use of terror, and the exploitation that is a permanent part of the colonial condition start to seem normal to them. That is the peaceful acceptance of colonialism's destructiveness that colonizers always strive for. But they never succeed.

It must be emphasized in light of Britain's colonies in Africa. The Labour government of 1945–1951 should have begun the process of decolonization, but due to ideological reasons (one only needs to read the Fabians' pronouncements), and especially because of the bloated persona of the foreign secretary Ernest Bevin, the majority of Labour parliamentarians were fiercely loyal to the empire, just as they are to the US and NATO today. Despite being pushed from India, they refused to take the teachings to heart. From the opposition benches, the diarist Chips Channon noted how enjoyable it was to hear Bevin, who sounded exactly like a Tory; in fact, Anthony Eden, Bevin's opponent, found it difficult to respond. When Churchill returned to Downing Street in 1951, the similarities in foreign policy between Labour and the Conservatives meant that he just carried on as before. Nothing needs to change.

All of Churchill's subsequent Colonial Office appointees, including Oliver Lyttleton, Alan Lennox-Boyd, and the despised pro-consul Evelyn ('Over-')Baring, believed that the main objective of imperial policy in Kenya was the establishment of yet another white settler state. The Rhodesian approach had been extremely effective and was simple to replicate. They did not factor in the mounting resentment of the Kikuyu, the group most negatively impacted, who by the middle of the 1950s numbered 1.5 million.

The settlers, whom they publicly referred to as "monkeys," became wealthy during the wartime commodities boom and rejected any proposal of a deal with "moderate African nationalists" (like Jomo Kenyatta). Kenya was a white-settler regime supported by British weapons under Churchill. The Kikuyu-led movement, known as Mau Mau by the oppressors, determined to launch an armed uprising to expel the British and their descendents from the nation and took oaths to that effect. The cattle of the settlers were stolen or destroyed, and the African accomplices received harsh treatment.

The Labour front bench continued to support the Churchill administration, but left-wing Labour figures like Barbara Castle, Fenner Brockway, and others involved in the Movement for Colonial Freedom started to strongly object. Lady Edwina Mountbatten insulted and humiliated the racist colonial secretary Oliver Lyttleton over the crimes in Kenya during a formal pre-coronation reception in 1953. Also present, her lover, Indian Prime Minister Jawaharlal Nehru, turned away from Lyttleton and departed the room. Churchill was informed by Lyttleton's complaint, and he gave the Foreign Office the order to forbid Edwina Mountbatten from traveling with her husband on an official tour to Turkey. Mountbatten disregarded the demand.

Churchill, Alan Lennox-Boyd, the governor of Kenya, Evelyn Baring, and Alan Lennox-Boyd, a personal favorite who was chosen for the Colonial Office after opposing Indian independence, were all staunch racists. Baring could have easily become an official in the Third Reich. In the eyes of Kenyan Africans, he was a violent thug who didn't only follow orders from London; he also anticipated them. The 1950s saw a rise in political opposition to the British, and those who founded the Mau Mau were no longer willing to put up with the level of violence meted out to their people. In retaliation, Baring established a network of prison camps much, far worse than anything Churchill had personally experienced during the Boer War in South Africa, with Churchill's support. Prisoners' accounts of their treatment resemble slave diaries. One survivor remarked, "It was like Hell on Earth." Elkins provides a summary of what took on both within and outside the camps: "Violence and torture had characterized camp life in Kenya for years. The communities were also hit by a wave of terror that included public cruelty, rape, and starvation, and thousands of people perished there.

One of the most pervasive illusions about the British Empire is that it was destroyed. Supporters of the story still compliment one another and ourselves on how good we were about it. Unlike the terrible French in Vietnam and Algeria, "We beat such a dignified retreat." The tragedy of Partition in India, which was covered up as unpleasant religions fighting one another, the violent suppression of the Malayan insurrection, and the vicious campaign against the freedom movement in Kenya are all kept out of the public eye. All of this is being called into question as historians from Africa, Asia, and portions of the US and UK dispel myths propagated by neo-imperial historians by highlighting the price paid in human lives to hasten decolonization.

Kenya had a series of organized crimes. Lennox-Boyd, Baring, and Churchill all escaped punishment.

Printed in Great Britain
by Amazon

35905648R10069